MW00908551

# UNSHACKLED

"Then you will know the truth,
and the truth will set you free."

Jesus in John 8 :32

# UNSHACKLED

A COLLECTION OF LIFE-TRANSFORMATION STORIES

VINITA SHAW

*Unshackled*
by Vinita Shaw

Copyright © 2017 by Vinita Shaw

To protect the identity of people, names have been changed.

All proceeds from this book will go for the work of
Disha Foundation : www.dishafoundationindia.in

All rights reserved.
No part of this publication may be reproduced, stored in a retrieval system,
or transmitted in any form or by any means—electronic, mechanical, digital,
photocopy, recording, or any other—except for brief quotations in printed
reviews, without prior permission of the publisher.

Published by
**VINITA SHAW**
44, Charak Sadan, Block - E
Vikaspuri
New Delhi - 18
Mobile: 9899304168
Email: unshackledtransformation@gmail.com


Cover design by Mrs Anjali John


Printed and bound in India by
GS Media, Secunderabad 500 067
E-mail: printing@ombooks.org

This book is dedicated to my mother, Mrs W. J. Missal
and
My husband, Pastor Timothy Shaw
for being a tremendous source of strength and encouragement to me

# CONTENTS

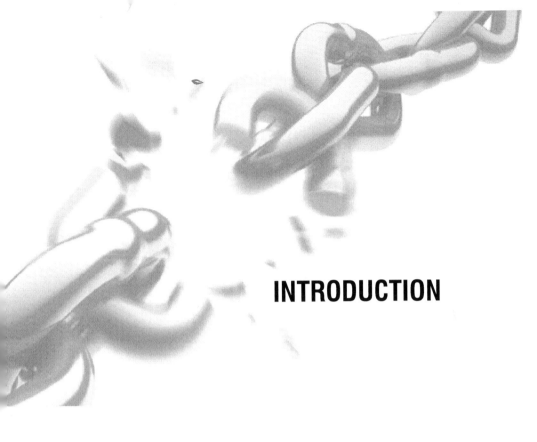

# INTRODUCTION

**The brutal gang rape** in the heart of the capital city of India had grabbed the eye-balls of the world's media. *"Nirbhaya"* was dying, although the pretense of her recovery was being put up. I knew she was as good as dead when she was shifted to a hospital in Singapore as the authorities did not want the country wide protests to get frantic and violent, furthermore.

It was a cold December night in 2012 in New Delhi, very close to Christmas and I lay snuggled in my warm bed, wide awake. The misogyny of India's mostly male and mostly rural politicians was on full display.

I cringed, helplessly from within, as warm angry tears spilled onto my pillow as I thought of the fury unleased against the girls and women of India.

Will these hate crimes against girls ever stop? What could I as an Indian woman do to stop this? I tossed and turned; miserably discouraged as sleep eluded me.

A few days later, *Nirbhaya* died, leaving behind a badly-shaken nation.

Eve Ensler, in A memory, a Monologue, a rant, and a prayer says, *"The mechanism of violence is what destroys women, controls women, diminishes women and keeps women in their so-called place."*

With my small team of friends, we were and continue to attempt to bring about a change in the mindset of millions who, to this day consider girl as bad luck, liability, a beast of burden and an object of show to be used, abused and refused.

What difference will our work make? I wonder.

Time has proved me wrong as these short stories are a testament to the transformation of individuals. These stories offer a glimpse into the daily lives of people who live in fear, misery, oppression, under the clutches of illiteracy, superstitions and mindsets set in stone, to be manipulated and cheated by the self-proclaimed holy men/women.

The inspiring journeys of these individuals to break-free from the shackles of culture, social and religious mindsets are worthy of applause as they face ostracism, yet march forward spreading the truth that has unshackled them.

The influence of women is helping girls to respect themselves and recognise their equal status along with their power to influence generations, the impoverished and unskilled women are finding new skills and financial independence, the possessed are being freed, the suicidal are finding hope, the lost are finding direction, those in darkness are seeing the light, and those who have been lied to, are finally discovering the truth.

The Bible is replete with the examples of girls and women have influenced decisions that have changed the course of History. Jesus, himself, used the influence of the Samaritan woman who became the first missionary and of Mary of Magdala whom He met first, after His resurrection.

Only, if we would comprehend this Truth, I pray.

Further, the reach of radio, in India, is stunning. Radio has a voice which reaches out and fills space without any visual distraction. It creates the illusion of community and a circle of trust, better than any other medium. Through radio there is a patient seeping of light into the dark and deep roots of ignorance.

In the last few years, through broadcasts like *Khush Khabri* (Hindi for good news), *Baat Pati ki* (Hindi for meaning matter of importance), *Aashar Alo* (Bengali for Ray of hope), *Disha* (Hindi for guidance), *Meri Awaz* (Hindi for My voice), *Satya Vachan* (Hindi for True words) and *Stuti Vandana* (Hindi for praise and Worship), we are beginning to see a glimmer of hope.

It is our constant endeavour to make our broadcasts more humane, full of relatable purpose and sincere intention.

The results are personal pains and dilemmas shared in total confidence seeking direction towards transformation.

It does not stop with individuals but further continues to balloon into networks who are agents of transformation in their respective areas of influence.

As the power of women's influence joins forces with radio outreaches, our prayer is that God would bless these individuals and make them into agents of transformation for their respective communities so that a Shining and United New India emerges.

As Mahatma Gandhi said, "Be the change you want to see in the world." May each of us be that change and God be our help.

Vinita Shaw
New Delhi, India

**1**

# BOLD AND BEAUTIFUL

*Hurting people gain a perspective that those who have not yet been hurt lack*

– Pastor Charles R. Swindoll

**Rani is bold** and beautiful. With short hair, dark red lipstick, five feet and five inches tall, she walks confidently with her head held high and is always on the go as she holds the hand of her daughter six year old daughter and moves effortlessly into the slums waving to the skinny and impoverished women who look at her with hope in their eyes.

With a loud and confident voice, Rani is far from being uncomfortable in the slums. I look at both of them as their faces shine and smile simultaneously, full of charm and grace.

Unbelievable! How can they smile? I wonder. Having gone through and still going through their valley of pain, how can a human heart take so much pain and yet have the ability to help others. My mind refuses to accept. Sleep continues to dodge me for many nights following my meeting with them.

Rani was discarded at birth by her doctor parents from Rajasthan, the desert state of India. The reason her faulty gender.

Raised by a Christian woman missionary, she grew up to marry a good man or so she thought or maybe he was. The early years of marriage were happy and a son was born. However, as the marriage grew in years, they grew apart. He had a habit of chasing women. As a faithful Indian woman, she confided in no one, rather put up a brave front and bore it all. All looked hunky-dory on the outside. Who would have guessed that she was living in hell?

One day her husband was arrested. He had been doing business with some goons and the whole gang was arrested. After months of running around, taking advice from lawyers and meeting judges, she was finally able to get him out on bail. However, he forgot all about her efforts and became more frustrated and abusive towards her. "*You are a worm from the dirty drain who was abandoned by her own mother"*. Physical and verbal torture became a routine with the add-on of his unfaithfulness.

Who could she confide in? She was an orphan and he was a powerful man. Moreover, she had learnt to hide her pain behind a cosmetic smile and make up. Due to her multiple surgeries, they could not have another baby. It would have to be only one son.

Reconciling to her fate, Rani continued to drudge through life posing as a happy and content house-wife and mother to their adult son. Rani was caught by surprise one day when she discovered a baby lying at her door step—a baby girl. Even the blood on her umbilical cord had not dried up yet. "Who could have possibly left a baby at her doorstep" she wondered to herself even as the compassion within her drowned all voices of doubt and sound reasoning. "My own childhood came back to me in a flash. Was not I too abandoned in the same manner by my biological parents," she said to herself. She took the baby in her arms and went to seek the permission of her husband to keep the baby. Her husband readily consented for her to keep the baby. She was overwhelmed with emotions and did not for once stop to wonder how her violent and abusive husband had given his consent so easily.

All Rani could think was that God had given her the same opportunity that the Christian missionary had when she raised Rani.

The passage of time revealed that the child was the product of her husband's unfaithfulness. For as the baby grew, the growing resemblance became apparent to one and all.

Daggers pierced her soul. But how could she abandon this child. The child was innocent. Nevertheless, she continued to love and nurture the child.

However, the violence her husband continued to inflict on her continued and a day came when she could take it no longer.

"If I stay with him, he will kill me with his physical, emotional and verbal torture," says Rani.

Today, Rani lives with her seven year old daughter, who is not her biological child, rather a daily reminder of her husband's unfaithfulness. She struggles with life depending on God and the love of her little one, whom she has ironically named Joy. Not only that, she has started a charity that offers assistance to victims of physical, mental and emotional women like herself.

In the midst of such of mental, emotional and physical pain, Rani reaches out to help other Indian women.

"It is only God who is sustaining us. I cry to Him. When I help them, I receive comfort. At least, I am able to help others. These women are my sisters in pain now."

As the women enter the room where we are talking, Rani smiles a bold and beautiful smile and beckons them to come in.

"Come on you brave women. We are going to stand together in our trials and God will be our help."

Will I ever forget meeting Rani and Joy? I do not think so!

# 2

# LOVE BLOSSOMS
# IN A BROTHEL

*Intelligence plus character—that is
the goal of true education.*

-MARTIN LUTHER KING JR.

**I could not** take my eyes off her. She was so good looking.
This was not the place for her to be in. Her fair complexion
and big black kohl lined eyes smiled as she spoke, revealing
an even set of teeth. She stood out of the group of girls with
her 5 feet 7 inches height.

I was visiting a shelter for rescued girls in Kolkota with
my team. All of them had horrid stories of their being sold

into sex slavery. It was poverty that had driven them thus far and they had ceased to trust any human being. Many were sold by their own family members.

The shelter provided them safe living, food and imparted skill-based training. Many of them had babies hanging to their small frames. Some of them were barely thirteen. Others needed little pups to love and cuddle and re-build their emotional life.

Many a times, a girl would go into a panic attack. The staff at the shelter was trained to deal with them. Many times even some of the staff would slip into depression because of their proximity with the victims. Special retreats were conducted to pray for them and encourage them in their work.

The girls showed us beautiful pieces of jewellery they had made with the raw material provided to them by the shelter authorities. Every morning they would come to learn the trade. An alternate employment opportunity was critical so they could feed themselves and their children who were born in the brothel.

Poonam came and shyly showed her craft to me. I looked at her and smiled. "Why don't you wear it and show me. It will look lovely on you," I encouraged her. She did so and smiled.

I asked her how she came to be here and this is what she told me.

"I come from the India-Bangladesh border area where there is a lot of poverty. There are no jobs there, so many people migrate. They come to Kolkata to pull rickshaws and work in factories or shops. My maternal Uncle brought me to Kolkata saying that he would get me a job. My parents did not have many options. With despair and fear in their eyes, they bid me goodbye as my Uncle took me from my village. I was all of fourteen years and understood that my younger siblings had to be fed.

After two days of bus journey, in the hot-humid weather of West Bengal, we came to Kolkata. I threw up all the way as I was not used to bus travel. I also cried. I had never been to a big city. It was throbbing with life. Crowds of people and lot of noise and heavy vehicles. Food markets and big shopping malls. It took some weeks for me to get used to it.

In Kolkata my Uncle sold me at a brothel. I have no idea as to how much money he sold me for. The Brothel *madam*, gave me new clothes and took me to a beauty parlour. I had no idea I could look so good. I was given good food and everybody was good to me.

I was like a goat being fattened for slaughter and totally oblivious, I realised later. On my sixteenth birthday, I was sent to a man and then began my time of horror. I could not believe what was happening. I cried and shouted but nobody came to my rescue.

One day, I got an opportunity to run away. I had learnt to use the bus, so I stole *madam's* telephone and fled. Soon after the bus took off, I received a call from *madam* asking me to come back or she would come to my village and tell my family about my work and nobody would let me enter my home. I disconnected her phone and kept moving.

After an hour or so of travel, I began to think of her threat. What if my parents do not let me in? Nobody would marry me anyway! Who would feed me? Here at least, I could earn money and send it back to my family. My life was ruined but I could protect my siblings. I could send them to school and give them a better chance at life. The stigma accompanied by threats from the pimps finally led me back to the red-light area.

I came to my senses and decided that if I have to sacrifice my life for the sake of my family, I will do it. And I came back to the brothel.

Years began to pass and it became a routine for me. I even had a son in the brothel. I had no regrets as I was able to send money to my family. With that money they got my sisters married and my brothers could receive an education. There were many other women like me. The brothel madam arranged for our children to be looked after. Young Christian girls and boys would come and play with our children and teach them songs, while we worked.

One day, Sanjay Babu came to the brothel. He was a drunkard who had lost faith in marriage because his wife had deserted him. He was a kind man and his gentleness attracted me to him. He was so different from the other men. Before we realised, we were hopelessly in love with each other. One day he asked me to come away with him.

He said, " Your son is growing up. What will you say to him?" He was right. So, I accepted the offer and we fled.

Today, Sanjay works as a chef. He cooks for us and sends my son to school. Then he sends me to this church shelter where I am learning to make jewellery and learning songs. There are mornings when I feel lazy. He forces me to get out of bed and sends me here, she says with a smile.

"Why don't you both get married?" I ask.

"Oh no, he has no faith in the institution of marriage. He says he will look after me and my son and in order to prove our love he doesn't think marriage is important. Even I agree with him because most of the men who come to the brothels are married and are being unfaithful to their wives. So what is marriage if we don't love and trust each other and look out for each other?"

I smile at her.

Suddenly, one of the girls in the shelter screamed and Poonam excused herself and ran to hold her. "This girl was sold by her own mother. She gets these panic attacks often. She is impossible to control. She has totally lost all faith in human beings, but I tell them my life-story and tell them to trust God. What He has done for me, He will do for them."

# 3

# NO MORE TEARS!

*I cried to the Lord and*
*He answered me by setting me free.*

- PSALM 118:5

**Phagun, a beautiful** fourteen year old came crying to me on the last day of the four-day excursion to the hills of North India. Ever since we started the trip, I had observed that she had been unusually quiet. I felt that she wanted to talk to me on many occasions but shied away because I was mostly surrounded by other girls. However, she finally approached me one day when she found me sitting alone under a flower-laden tree. With tear-filled eyes, she told me:

23

"My mom's sister and her husband live in our small house along with their baby. My parents love me to bits and so do my aunt and uncle, but for the last few months, I have been noticing a strange behaviour on the part of my uncle.

"Each time he finds me alone, he tries to touch me and hold me. In the beginning, I thought he was being playful but having heard your talk on how careful we need to be as girls, I have understood that he had been misbehaving with me. I am so scared of him now that I even avoid having meals with the family. I don't know if my mother will believe me or not. What if my mom gets angry with me or my uncle leaves my aunt and goes away? I fear for the little baby too. But if I do not stop him now, he will do the same mischief with his own daughter." Phagun wept inconsolably as she poured out her heart to me.

I hugged her, and then I praised her for being so brave and sharing her fearful concerns with me. My advice to her was this: "Please share this with your mother, and if she does not believe you, I will talk to her. It is not your fault, and you do not have to worry about your aunt and uncle. If I make one phone call to the police, your uncle will be in prison for molesting a minor. Go and tell your mother this. The law is very strong, and I am standing with you."

That was enough. Phagun told her mother, and her mother took immediate action. She confronted the couple who immediately left their house. Phagun is safe now and is happily growing and learning.

In many cases, parents do not believe their children and even if they do, they force the child into silence and then into abortion, thereby damaging the minor girl for her entire life.

In millions of families in India, girls are as unsafe in their homes as they are outside their homes. In a recent case, a fourteen year old was raped repeatedly and finally forced to drink acid mixed with coke, which led to her death; this is just a peek into the realities of daily living for little Indian girls. Something similar could have happened to Phagun too but for the awareness and timely counselling that she received.

Now, Phagun happily shares with her classmates about "good-touch" and "bad-touch" and how to raise their voices and share their predicaments to bring the perpetrators to book.

"Do not think that it is your fault—that's a lie. You must raise your voice and let people know the truth," Phagun exhorts her classmates.

# 4

# SWEET SIXTEEN

*Give a girl an education and introduce her
properly into the world, and ten to one,
she has the means of settling well, without
further expense to anybody.*

-JANE AUSTEN

**"Mother, Mother,** I got a marriage proposal from one of
my relatives in the USA? But I said no," gushed Bulbul in her
typical warm, loud, and chirpy manner, beaming from ear
to ear.

"Why would you do that?" I asked, feigning ignorance.

"Well, I remember all that you taught me. So, I want to finish my education, become financially independent, and then get married. Moreover, I am only sixteen. I am a minor."

My eyes moistened with tears on hearing Bulbul's words. It was one of those moments when I realized how deeply I could influence the minds and hearts of these young girls.

"But why would you do that? Who would say no to a marriage proposal from a man who lives in America. So many young girls dream of going to America," I teased.

Bulbul laughed revealing her perfect set of teeth; she knew very well that I was testing her and said, "No, Mother, I want to be a police officer. I don't want to be dependent on my husband for my financial needs."

Bulbul was always ahead of the other girls. She stood out with her beautiful smiling face and dancing brown eyes. She was always good at studies and topped consistently; she did not like coming second in class. I remember once during a tailoring class competition, she stood second; she did not take it well. Her large light-brown eyes quickly turned into a pool of tears. I had to hug her and encourage her to take things in her stride.

In every class, be it a value education class or a special session on law and the protection of girls, she would be very attentive; she was often the first to answer questions. So much so that I had to ask her to be quiet so that the other girls in the group would be encouraged to speak and develop their confidence. A keen learner of the English language, she regularly practiced her communication skills. However, Bulbul came from a disturbed family—her mother had been married thrice.

The disturbances in family life had forced the mother to leave Bulbul and her siblings in the hostel. Their childhood was marked by uncertainty and want. The mother worked at a petrol pump in extremely vulnerable circumstances where it was normal for the manager to ask female employees for sexual favours.

Despite all these handicaps, Bulbul became a keen learner over the years. Be it at the workshops we conducted to create social awareness and the risks of abortion on a woman's health or the dances and the dramas in which we taught the girls to speak on the radio and write dramas and poems, Bulbul would participate eagerly.

After finishing grade 10, she secured a seat in an English-medium school along with her younger sister. Not only did she work hard herself, but she also encouraged her younger sister to do the same. Today, Bulbul is a source of encouragement to many youngsters. She is often invited to give interviews on radio broadcasts to inspire girls of her age to study and become self-reliant.

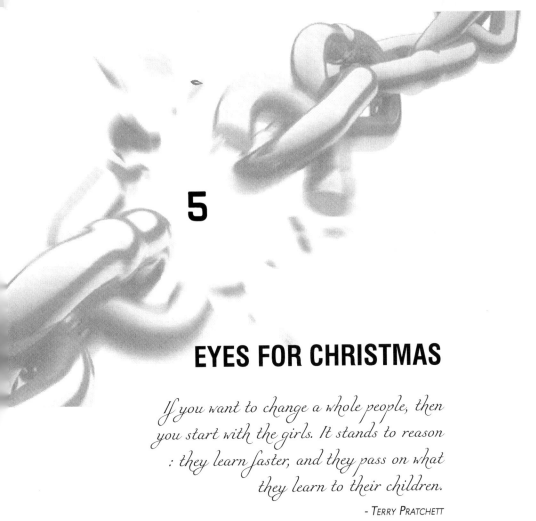

# 5

# EYES FOR CHRISTMAS

*If you want to change a whole people, then
you start with the girls. It stands to reason
: they learn faster, and they pass on what
they learn to their children.*

- TERRY PRATCHETT

**I remember** the first time I set my eyes on Megha. All of five years old, she was a new admission to the hostel. "Is she from Afghanistan?" I enquired looking at her milky white complexion, light-brown eyes, and long lashes as she shyly shook hands with me.

"Why is she here?" I whispered to the warden as I tried to make Megha feel welcome.

"Her parents are middle aged now. Her father and mother have families of their own with adult children. They came together for some years, but once Megha was born, they went back to their own respective families. Nobody wants Megha now."

I grimaced.

Each time the school would close and guardians/single parents would come to take their wards for a few days to their slum settlements, Megha refused to go.

"My mother curses me day in and day out and wishes I were dead. I am not able to finish my homework. I want to stay here," Megha often complained to the warden.

On her sixth birthday, the warden called Megha's father and asked him to visit her as was the custom with other girls too. Surprisingly, Megha's father gave a very shocking response. He said, "We do not celebrate the birthdays of girls in our family," and he abruptly disconnected the phone.

This was when we decided to celebrate the birthdays of our girls every month. We bought cakes, balloons, and decorations, and the girls whose birthdays fell in that month would receive special gifts, special attention, cakes and goodies. Not only did this make them feel important, but it also gave them the understanding that they are precious to God and to us. The objective of the birthday celebrations was to rid these young girls of poor self-worth. From childhood, these girls are tutored to believe that they are worthless.

As Megha entered her teens, a friend in the hostel discovered that she was losing her eyesight very rapidly. She would keep squinting while talking and would hold the book very close to her eyes. We took her to the doctor for a check up; it was discovered that both her eyes would require surgery and special lenses had to be fitted or else she would go blind.

When the parents were informed, they quickly washed their hands off. "I cannot see myself. What will I do for her?" growled Megha's unconcerned mother.

Nevertheless, we went ahead and performed Megha's eye surgery at the best government hospital in New Delhi. Megha wanted to join in the Christmas party at the hostel but she could not because her discharge from the hospital was scheduled for a week after Christmas. Therefore, we went to visit her with her cake and gifts; Megha was ecstatic. True to her nature, she shared the cake with the doctors and nurses who had cared for her. Megha might have missed the Christmas party in the hostel but she received an invaluable Christmas gift: her eyes. Other than that, Megha now knows that she is a unique creation of God loved by Him and precious to Him. Not inferior to anyone.

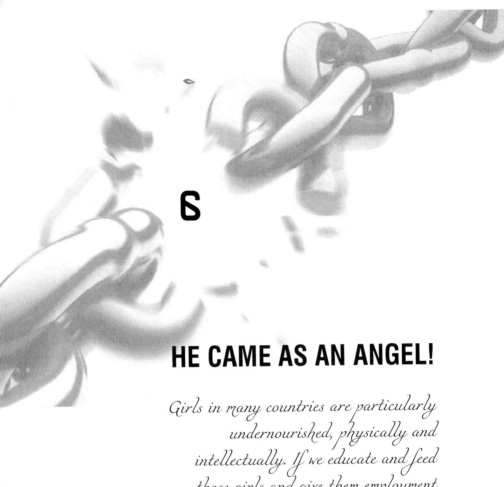

# 6

# HE CAME AS AN ANGEL!

*Girls in many countries are particularly undernourished, physically and intellectually. If we educate and feed those girls and give them employment opportunities, then the world as a whole will gain a new infusion of human intelligence.*

**Poshi is one** of our not-so-bright girls who managed to secure admission in an English-medium school after studying in a Hindi-medium, government-aided school. For 10 years, she lived in a boarding school where she learnt English communication and tailoring skills.

35

"Each child has unique gifts and is precious in the sight of God, be it a girl or a boy. Do not believe the lies that our culture teaches us saying that girls are inferior to boys." This is what we teach the children who come to our hostel.

Poshi's gift of tailoring was discovered when she was quite young. During the long, hot summer vacations, we made all kinds of activities and indoor games an integral part of our training. Of particular interest to the girls were the "boot camps" for which we invited subject specialists; these specialists taught the girls various crafts, tailoring, hair dressing and make up, operating computers, and cooking. After the girls discover their specific area of interest, we provide them with higher levels of training in that skill. Most girls usually make a career out of what they learn at the hostel.

Poshi's mother had abandoned her and her sister for another man. Her father, a driver, brought them to the hostel; he visited them once in a while. Poshi was a quiet girl. A slow learner, she was weak at studies and easily burst into tears. However, her tailoring skills left us quite dumbfounded, and before we realized it, she was designing and making full dresses. In no time, she began making gowns and was keen to pursue fashion designing.

Today, Poshi lives with her elder sister who works at a call center. Whenever Poshi gets some time off her studies, she works on the sewing machine that we provided her and makes some pocket money. Recently, she shared her story with us.

"I had gone to the doctor along with my father to treat my dental problem. While we awaited our turn, an elderly man sitting next to me casually asked me what I did. A red alert went up in my mind because you have taught us that it is a big, bad world out there, and we needed to be careful. But I thought it safe to respond to this man because my father was sitting next to me and this man was quite old. We made some conversation in English, and he was very impressed. He told me about himself and how he and his wife ran a foundation to help economically weak girls to become financially independent. He asked what I would like to do in my life and offered to help with books and stationery. He asked for my telephone number, which I gave.

A few days later, he began to message me and invite me home to collect books and stationery. When I said that I would come with my father, he said, I could bring my other classmates as well. "Why bother father?" I thought. I said that I would let him know. He texted me again after some time and said that I should not be too serious about my studies and should have some fun with boys as well. I ignored him but he continued to persist, and shortly afterwards, he began sending me lewd messages. I got very scared. I had thought he was an angel, but he turned out to be the devil himself. It was very difficult to shake him off. But after turning him down many times, he stopped."

"So, what have you learned from this experience?" I asked.

"Never to trust anyone however sweet talking he or she may be."

I reminded Poshi of the session a High Court lawyer had taken for our girls; the lawyer had said, "Please beware of Uncles and Aunties who come with sweet talk to you. Even if these people are known to you, they could be child traffickers."

Today, Poshi is wiser and has found her voice as well as her courage. She travels to school in the city bus, not fearfully but with her head held high. Her walk shows that she is a force to reckon with. The once shy and gullible Poshi is now vocal and enlightens other girls to be cautious and not be taken for a ride by sweet-talking and innocuous-looking men and women.

# 7

# GORGEOUS UNDER COVER!

*When I come to the end of my rope, God is there to take over.*

**As the Doctor** held the foetal model and showed pictures on the screen of a fully formed baby at twelve weeks in the womb, her jaw dropped and her eyes became pools of water. Her eyes were glued to the instruments that the doctor showed. Tools used to tear foetuses to pieces. Jameela, as we got to know later had been forced into having multiple abortions by her husband and the trauma of all she had undergone spilled forth as she wept. She was not alone. There were many women and girls in the room who were hearing the truth about abortion for the first time. Stunned silence and tears quickly replaced the laughter and chatter.

Who would believe that there is actually another very narrow lane running behind the narrow roads of a large city. I would have never guessed, because the narrow roads with traffic congestion is bad enough. On the invitation of a local partner, I found myself and my team follow the partner into that very narrow lane at the entrance of which is a men's urinal. A strong Muslim woman led us. Her name is Majida, a single Muslim woman from a very impoverished family has grown, in the last 30 years, to become a force to be reckoned with when it comes to the community work among Muslim women. On her invitation, we organised a health seminar and taught about women reproductive issues with emphasis on abortion. Carrying with us foetus models and taking along our Lady gynaecologist, one by one, we squeezed past the tightly packed houses and into the centre where more than a hundred young women awaited us.

As more women entered, I was taken aback as they quickly got rid of their *burqa* (the long black shroud with a veil) through which only their eyes visible. Under the *burqa* were henna coloured hair with different hairstyles, dark red lipsticks and attractive clothes. They were quite a talkative bunch, giggling and talking simultaneously. All the women were learning a skill at this center: either tailoring, embroidery, computer or beauty and make up or hair styling.

We were surprised at the way they participated in discussions about the status of women in our country and found them to be very well informed.

However, as our gynaecologists began to show slide after slide of the baby's development in the womb, I sat and observed each one. The young, unmarried ones listened with keen interest but there were a few married ones whose eyes filled with tears as they realised that they had been misinformed into believing that the foetus in their womb was just a clump of tissue (they told us later). They had never heard of this knowledge before.

As the time came for picture booklets of life in the womb to be distributed, they all jumped. Each one wanted to take it back home to show their husband and family that foetus was no clump of tissue but a fully formed human being.

*"Please give us these booklets so we can take them home to show to our husbands. We have never seen pictures of baby in the womb and this will deter us from doing this heinous crime again in the future,"* was the united chorus they all sang.

"Also, go and share this information with all those you know. Unknowingly, you are committing a grave sin by killing the unborn child. This is murder. Go and tell as many people as you possibly can," says Majida in her typical loud and coarse voice to which all the women responded in affirmative.

# 8

# HELP YOURSELF

*Social entrepreneurs are not content just to give a fish or teach how to fish. They will not rest until they have revolutionized the fishing industry*

-BILL DRAYTON

**Rita is all** of sixteen years, with a frail body and small voice. Her large eyes on her oval-shaped face beam as she shows me the beautiful cards.

"You are so gifted," I exclaim.

"We learnt it all here at the hostel. Thank you for teaching us all this."

I look at her. How many come back to thank, I wonder. Very rarely and here she is expressing her gratitude.

"Will you share your family tragedy on the radio interview so girls and women can take strength and find their feet, in the midst of daunting challenges that stare at them?" I ask.

" Yes, definitely!" she quips.

This is her story in her own words.

"We all lived in a joint family near the foothills of Nainital. My mother is very beautiful. My father's family loved for her gentle and caring nature, her and tried to protect her but my father was mad every time a daughter was born. He would beat her mercilessly.

I remember being terrified, weeping and hiding behind the curtain. There was little one could do. Even the neighbours didn't pay attention as they were used to domestic violence. "It is his woman; he can do with her as he pleases."

My grandmother used to offer all kinds of prayers in the temple, so a son would be born.

Each time my mother got pregnant, my father would cease beating her, in the hope that she would finally birth to a son.

However, every time it was a girl. Finally, after the birth of three daughters, my father lost his mind.

He just dragged my mother out of the bed with us clinging to her and banged the door on our faces.

My mother fainted in pain and weakness. We had nowhere to go. A kind neighbour's wife took us in for a couple of days.

My grandparents' house was closed as they had taught my mother that, after marriage the husband's home is a woman's home and her parents are as good as dead. She can never come back.

My mother believed every word to the letter.

Having nowhere else to go, she got onto a city bus with the three of us. On the bus she met an elderly man, who looking at our condition enquired, "Where is their father?"

My mother broke down and told the whole story.

The man took pity on us and took us to his house in the city.

He was a kind man. A widower. He had adult children who were married and had their own lives. He lived alone. He invited my mother to live with him. We got a new father.

My younger sister and I were admitted in a Christian hostel, while the youngest remained with our mother. Soon she joined us too. Our new father and mother lived in the house and my mother took care of everything. He even allowed her to get the training of a mid-wife so she could fend for herself, should the need arise.

Years went by. My father used to come and visit us with gifts and good food every month. We studied very hard and did well in studies.

All through these years, my mother had refused to marry this kind man because of the trauma she had. She lived like a wife but did not wish to be tied down in marriage. After showing much patience, one day the elderly man got very angry with my mother and drove her out of his house. He also stopped visiting us and giving us money.

We were back to square one.

The only difference was that by then, I had turned sixteen years old and my younger sisters, fourteen and twelve respectively.

My mother rented a very small room in the big city. She began travelling as and when she was invited to serve as a mid-wife.

Today, the responsibility of taking care of our little home, my younger sisters, as well as studying is all on my shoulders.

I try to help my mother earn a living even as I study. I am very good at art and craft, makeup and hair dressing-all of which I learnt at the hostel.

We are pained because of the way our society has treated us. We feel helpless but we have been taught to become self-reliant and independent.

We want to grow up to be a blessing to our mother and help change the mind-set that our society has against girls and women. We want to prove to the world that we are not in any way inferior and that we deserve equal status.

We are very grateful to God for helping us understand the truth that girls and boys are made in His image and are equally precious to Him.

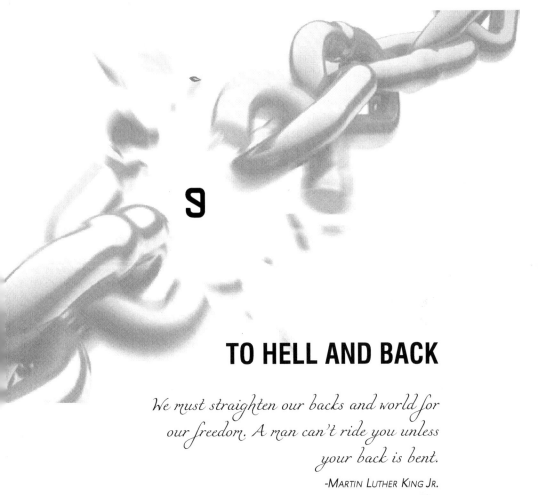

**9**

# TO HELL AND BACK

*We must straighten our backs and world for*
*our freedom. A man can't ride you unless*
*your back is bent.*

-MARTIN LUTHER KING JR.

**Be it an illegitimate** teenage boy who is suicidal, or a woman considering abortion, or an abused wife, Malini has love, patience and a word of counsel for each of them.

With her comforting words of wisdom and prayers, she leads many out of a life of depression and misery to a life of hope in Christ.

Meet Malini, our senior counselor.

"It is believed that if a girl has suffered in her parents' home, she will have a good time at her husband's home, but in my case, I suffered in both places", says Malini, one of our radio counselors, even as her nose becomes slightly pink and eyes moisten.

Malini hails from a small village in the city of Allahabad, Uttar Pradesh. Majority of the people there are Hindus, but somehow her father wanted to marry a Christian girl. He had met a group of Christians somewhere and was strongly influenced to marry one. Since in the village, a girl of his liking was not found, he was introduced to an orphan girl from Gorakhpur who had been raised by British missionaries. He knew nothing of her background. Was she born an orphan or like so many girls there, been abandoned.

The initial years were happy. They had seven children. Malini's father went to work and her mother stayed at home to take care of the children. All the children were sent to school. The older ones grew up and got married.

One day her father suddenly died, leaving behind a grieving, helpless widow who had four little ones to take care of. The married ones were least interested in pitching in.

Malini's mother tried to cook and clean in other people's homes and take tuitions, but it was not enough to make ends meet. Soon one by one the children had to drop out of school.

The relatives wanted to nothing to do with a widow and her brood of impoverished children.

One day, Malini's mother met an old hostel girl with whom she had grown up. They were like sisters. The friend took the family in.

Little Malini did not know that her mother was now the live in partner of her friend's husband.

"I look back and think now. I did not understand why Uncle took care of us, why he brought groceries and was kind to us. Why my mom disappeared with him behind a closed door as the aunt looked away without any reaction."

Her young mind carries images, but the understanding came much later.

Today, she understands that her helpless mother and equally helpless aunt had to give in to the whims and fancies of the man who gave them food, shelter and security. Any kind of protest could result in them being evicted—fearing which both gave in.

Life was difficult for Malini as she was bundled from one family's home to another. She fails to recollect the number of houses she lived in.

"I was made to do all the household chores while their children studied. I was scolded and misunderstood. Every night, I cried myself to sleep."

As she entered teenage, her mother called her home and that is when her Uncle began to show special interest in her. "Why is this little girl always misunderstood?" he would lovingly fondle her head. Hungry for love, Malini felt loved and cared for till one day she was rudely awakened by him as he fondled her young body.

She froze!

Her mind refused to comprehend. The shock was too much to take in.

Was it affection? No, this was not right!

She pushed him away and ran out of the house.

She does not remember how many sleepless nights she spent hiding and protecting herself from the very man who was the benefactor of their family.

Malini's mother decided to get her married at the age of fifteen.

Her married sister brought a young boy and proposed for Malini to marry him. Malini had nowhere to turn to. Months later she met a Pastor and wife with whom she shared her family situation and who took pity on her and got her admitted in a Christian boarding school. She finished her studies and went back home, where again she was at high risk.

Finally, a man proposed to for her marriage and in order to escape her fate, Malini married him hoping that her new life would end her misery. But she was wrong.

Marriage brought further misery. Her husband was abusive and had extramarital affairs, including with her own elder sister.

Terrorised of her husband's wrath, she was forced to accept the multiple partners he had.

However, there is one thing that she did not give up on; praying to Jesus and going to Church. Somehow her husband did not stop her. Perhaps he thought, being a member of a church meant the boys would secure admission in good Christian schools and later colleges.

Malini continued to faithfully follow Christ and lead many women to Him.

One day, her husband said to Malini, " Do you know that if I don't feed you, you are going to die of hunger."

Malini wept before the Lord.

Truly, she was not self-sufficient. She always had to ask him for money and live like a servant.

The next day, she received a call from a non profit based in New Delhi offering her the position of a Telephone counselor.

Today, Malini is busy receiving phone calls of with the listeners who call in day and night. She prays for them and counsels them. Her husband supports her in her household chores.

"The whole scenario has turned upside down", beams a happy Malini as she continues to use her power to influence the listeners who call in, showing them the way out of darkness and despair.

# 10

# ABANDONED

*Empowered women empower women.*

**Our little team** was on a visit to an elderly care home. It was Christmas time. The special time of the year when the Church calendar was abuzz with celebrations and social outreaches. The markets filled with Christmas decorations and cakes.

The objective of the visit to the old people's home was to sensitize the children about caring for the under-privileged.

We were carrying with us a full year's groceries, goodies, cakes and warm clothes.

The children were excited at the thought of the outing. We had plans to sing carols and spend time with the elderly inmates.

All twenty of them were waiting for us. Cuddled in warm clothes, they were sitting by the fire. As one by one, the children shook hands and exchanged hugs with them, they blessed the children.

One child asked, "Where is that aunty who gets mad during the full moon time?"

"Oh, she is alright today. Just does not like to mingle with people. She likes to keep to herself," the warden informed.

"Can we see her?" and without waiting for a response from the warden, they ran up the stairs to meet Dorris.

Unkempt hair and wild eyes, Dorris, sat in a corner of the corridor.

"She does not listen to any one except me", said the Warden who tried patted Dorris, reassuring her that the children had come to wish her Merry Christmas.

But Dorris felt uneasy. She shrieked and shouted, till the terrified youngsters scurried like fearful rats, all tumbling down the stairs.

"We had found her looking for food in the garbage dump. She comes from a very well to do family. The dogs had bitten her and she had a deep steel bangle embedded in her wrist. With great difficulty, we had it removed."

"Was she born mad?", someone asked.

"Oh, no. She is one of six children. Her father was a very rich businessman. They were the richest in the colony. They had a car in those days. Dorris must have been about fourteen years old. A happy child, so we are told by the people who knew her family. She used to go to school and did well in studies. During those days, there were a lot of anglo-Indians left behind after the British left India. Dorris was trained to sing and dance by an anglo-Indian dance teacher.

She even had a couple of boys down the lane vying for her attention, as happens with every teenager.

Dorris lost her mind when one day she returned from school. It was like any other regular day. Always in a hurry, she rushed into her house to see what was cooked. They had a train of servants. Her mother used to supervise them. There was a party that night. Dorris heard her mother crying. Lately, the rows between her father and mother were becoming intense. Her elder siblings had little care for her and no time to worry about what was happening between their parents. But Dorris, being the youngest and of sensitive nature, was bothered by it. This time the row sounded worse than before.

"I will not tolerate your affairs any more", her mother yelled at the Father who was slightly drunk as usual. Most of the times silent, her father was an anglo-Indian and smoked cigars. But that day, he was red-faced as he staggered out of the bedroom.

Dorris had not imagined in her wildest dreams what followed next and it was then that she lost her mind. Dorris saw her father light a match to her mother's beautiful embroidered red nylon sari. It was like a silent movie as

Dorris watched, her mother shell shocked, her father speechless.

Then began the violent screaming of her mother. In front of her eyes, Dorris saw her mother burn to death. Even as the servants scurried into the room with buckets of water, at the risk of invoking the wrath of the Sahib.

Dorris's mother's nylon sari very quickly lapped up her beautiful flesh, till no sound came from her.

Dorris fainted.

When she woke up, she saw her father being escorted out of the beautiful red brick house they had lived for as long as her memory served her. The gorgeous bouganvillias and the well-tended gardens soon became a distant memory as she was escorted to her neighbour's home for food and bath.

It was the last time people saw Dorris as a sane person.

She used to babble, scream and fight with people. Who was there to look after her. She used to be mad at her siblings. She was traumatised. After many vain attempts, they left her behind and migrated. She was left at the mercy of the colony's neighbours who had known the family and due to their good relations in the past, let Dorris roam about.

But as time passed and Delhi became Delhi NCR, one by one those who knew Dorris passed away or sold their homes to move away, Dorris became an orphan in the real sense of the word.

The beggars' children threw stones at her and the dogs barked at her, since she wanted a share of their food.

It was then that we found her, heard her story and brought her here. We tended her wounds, and gave her a room of her own. She cannot tolerate any one sharing a room with her and likes to stay by herself.

"I wonder what will happen to her, after I am gone"'", says the warden who is like a mother to Dorris.

Somehow, the warden has managed to restore Dorris' faith in humankind."

The warden patted Dorris lovingly and offered her a piece of cake. Dorris took it, while giving us a hostile look.

"Go away", she said even without mouthing the words.

We hugged the warden and gave her Christmas greetings.

"You are doing a great job here. God bless you and may you continue to bring love and hope to all these elders who have been rejected by family and society." We blessed her as we bid adieu to the rest of the elderly, who also had poignant stories to tell.

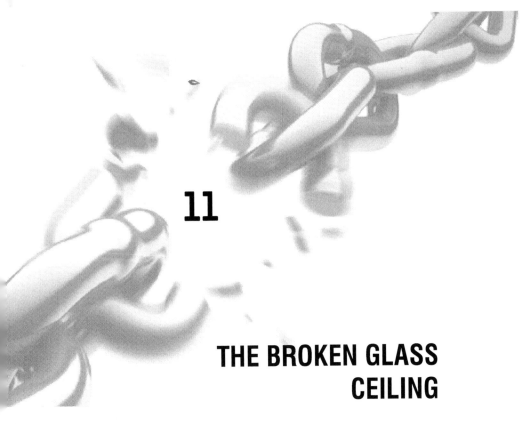

# 11

# THE BROKEN GLASS CEILING

*Reasonable people adapt themselves to the world. Unreasonable people attempt to adapt the world to themselves. All progress, therefore, depends on unreasonable people.*

-GEORGE BERNARD SHAW

**The horror** of that night continues to haunt me to this day. Many years have elapsed since, but there isn't a single day my mind doesn't walk down that painful memory lane where I was left bleeding, dying, battered and broken to be publicly humiliated and blamed even though I was the victim.

It was November, the onset of winter. A very pleasant month in Delhi.

It was past 10.30 p.m. and I was sitting in my CEO office waiting for the verdict as the Governing Board met to work on the action plan for my removal. The meeting had begun at 9 a.m.

I waited with my team or who I thought was my team, memories of twenty years gone by filled my mind, one by one.

My life with this international organisation had been one painful episode after another. Nevertheless, this was the climax.

It had been a long haul for me. I had joined the organisation leaving behind a promising publishing career to serve God. I had grown with it and loved it till the time it became a part of me.

A telephone ringing in the secretary's office brought me back to the present reality.

Whatever would happen, I was calm and poised and would remain that way. No matter what, I would not break down in public is a promise I had long made to myself as I lived in a world of men where my meekness was often mistaken as my weakness and my patience as timidity.

Things had taken a nasty turn soon after the Board decided to renew my three years term and extend it to 5 years. From day one as a woman CEO, I had sensed a resentment in the men who reported to me. After all, I had replaced an elderly man who was known for his maverick ways of operating. People shivered with fear every time he walked into the office building.

When it was time for him to hand over the reins to me, these were his words said to me in his office, "I will never hand over the organisation to a woman."

His angry loud voice had been accompanied with a file that he threw angrily in my direction which landed noisily on the marble floor.

At the age of 39, I was appointed the CEO of this international organisation. There never had been a female CEO before; in any of the countries where the organisation had its operations.

The first year had been shaky and I found much non-co-operation but as I began to travel around and patiently connect with the staff, my inter-personal skills helped in binding the wounds of the era gone by. Found to be doing well with cost effective measures in the face of economic recession, transparency with the sponsors and introducing best financial practices, the Board had decided to give me a five years extension. To show their appreciation, they also gave me a handsome performance allowance.

What happened soon after was like a bolt from the blue. Some senior male staff rallied some unhappy staff together to write against me to the international office who believed them. The Indian board bowed under international pressure. As for my team members, they were just so happy with the decision because they were vying for the position themselves.

A banging on my door rudely jolted me out of my thoughts and as I gathered my thoughts which lay strewn around, I looked up.

I was being summoned to the board room.

Before a full board, the woman chairman addressed me asking me to step out of the CEO office and proceed on a three months sabbatical.

No explanations were offered.

No consolation.

No words of advice.

Did I take it lying down? No, I did not. I left behind a divided board, with half of them resigning with immediate effect alongwith me and a weeping female chairperson who had bowed to the patriarchal mindset after being offered a position on the international Board with free air tickets for her family travel.

As I walked out boldly with a smile om my face, my team member gave me the Judas kiss and hugged me.

The typical Indian way; what a woman thinks or speaks is of no consequence because woman in India is the second sex, with limited spaces, only to be seen, never to be heard.

A country where the emotions of a woman hold little value.

Was I surprised at my fate? No, not really because discrimination is something I have experienced since my childhood. My parents were pitied because they had produced three daughters of which I was the eldest. An acute consciousness about my gender leading to inferiority complex had hence driven me to refuse initially when the international office had asked me to take on the CEO position. "Please get an Indian man as a CEO", I had told them.

Many of my men friends have asked me, " Would they have dared behave like this with a man? He would have taken them to court and ensured the organisation was reported to the government."

One prominent government minister had remarked at a public meeting, " We are democracy and even the worst of criminal with all the evidences in place is given a fair trial."

Fair trial, what's that? I am an Indian woman.

Bruised, broken and battered, it was no less than a gang-rape. The public humiliation, the questions and the smirks followed and all blamed me. Some vocalised; others did not.

As usual, it is the victim that is blamed.

"You should have been smarter."

"You should have not resigned"

"You should have taken them to court"

I gave myself time to heal. As they say, "You do not learn as much as you go up the ladder as you learn while you are coming down."

Finally, I got up. It had to be a self-help, I realized. Family and friends could go only up to a certain extent. I had to make the effort to get up which I finally did.

I looked a good look at myself. I was all of 45 years of age, had an excellent track record and was well-travelled. I also had the skills of speaking and writing. And I had given myself an year long well-deserved rest during which I had taken to reading writing and travelling.

I decided then. I would speak and write for those who cannot.

I would become their voice.

Not only my writings proved to be therapeutic but my campaigns for gender-equality have ballooned. More and more girls and women across India are becoming agents of transformation and influencing their families, societies and the nation at large.

# 12

## SOWING HOPE

*Consider the costs of allowing half a country's human resources to go untapped. Women and girls cloistered in huts, uneducated, unemployed, and unable to contribute significantly to the world represent a vast seam of human gold that is never mined.*

-NICHOLAS D. KRISTOF AND SHERYL WUDUNN IN HALF THE SKY, HOW TO CHANGE THE WORLD.

**"Lazish, open your** mouth and speak clearly into the microphone," exhorted the coordinator of our women's skill training program. She had brought along a few girls to the radio station so that they could share the details of their journey from financial dependence to independence. The girls had been trained to speak clearly and were now speaking their parts on the radio, albeit nervously.

"Never mind, not a problem," I encouraged them. "First timers do get nervous in recording studios when they start speaking into the microphone. It's alright to be nervous. Have some water please."

Lazish, kept her gaze fixed on me as I spoke. "Speak Lazish, speak, you know what you have to say," said the coordinator once again trying to encourage the girl. But no matter how many times we tried, Lazish would not speak. After a while, she quietly left with her coordinator and the other women.

Where had I found Lazish? Why could she not speak? Here is her story.

Three years back, our attention was drawn to a slum cluster in the heart of the capital city of New Delhi. We received a distress call from a center:

"Please come and help our women. They will remain helpless if you do not teach them any skills. Girls are as unsafe inside their homes as they are outside. Minor girls getting pregnant is the norm here and the government-appointed family counselors are quick to suggest abortions. A shroud of silence covers them, as black as the veils they wear."

I vividly remember my first visit to this slum cluster. I was greeted by the stench emanating from a men's urinal.

I passed by a veritable zoo from where emerged a pig that looked like it had freshly rolled in dirt; there was an old cow, a measly looking cat, and a couple of stray dogs. Rodents scurried around even as crows noisily gathered at the periphery of a rubbish dump—all feasting on the open garbage littered all across the narrow slippery lane that opened into this large urban slum.

"We have requested the local counselor to get it cleaned. But you know how things move when the economically weak are involved," said the local project coordinator apologetically. We covered our faces and walked past the open drains into the slum settlement that housed approximately 70,000 inhabitants, predominantly Muslims with a scattering of some Hindu low-caste families.

The languid stares of men greeted us as they hung around outside their shanty homes while some men bathed outside clad in their loincloths. A peek inside the small space they called home was enough to make anyone wonder how families of eight to ten members could squeeze in and live together. The colony dwellers are used to our visits, and I can almost hear them thinking, "These stupid women and their stupid ambitions to help other women!"

The disdain in their eyes and the smirk on their lips cannot discourage me and my band of women. I can see where the frustration stems from. Most of them are immigrants working as casual laborers and rickshaw pullers; they have hordes of children and alcoholism is rampant among them. Many are even drug peddlers and traffickers; each one is trying to eke out a living, by hook or by crook. Domestic violence and abuse in their families is the norm.

I shook myself out of my deep thoughts as I heard the excited chatter of the young women who had come to greet us with shy yet happy faces even as I grimaced and avoided an injured dog that had come to sniff at me: "Please take away the dog. I am scared." I smile, and those around me laughed as they drove away the poor animal. Then, they led us into a nice, clean, and freshly swept center provided by the government to our partner organization.

Women come to this center daily. One woman said, "It's like a second home for us. We like to hang around her, chat, learn, play, and go home only when we have to." For the last three years, girls have been coming here to learn skills that will help them earn a living. They are offered classes in computers, tailoring, and beauty/hair styling.

Lazish was one of the girls coming to this center. Her pale face almost made her look anaemic although she had a heavy build. She was the eldest of five sisters and two brothers. Her father, a rickshaw puller and the only breadwinner of the family, suffered from a paralytic attack and had been bed ridden for the last two years.

Lazish could have been an easy prey for human traffickers. Girls are often kidnapped and sold in cities where they do not know the language. When such things happen, the parents mourn for some time and then come to terms with the situation. If they go to the police, they are sent away saying that their daughter must have run away with some guy. Therefore, to save face, many do not even register a complaint with the police.

A few months after Lazish's father was taken ill, her mother realized that in order to get food in their stomachs, Lazish would need some training. So, one day, she brought the very shy 16-year-old Lazish to the center. "We have no money and nowhere to go. Please help us before we die of hunger. All have turned their backs on us."

It was then that the coordinator enrolled Lazish as a student in the tailoring and beautician's course. Lazish also started learning English. Painfully and slowly, Lazish started coming out of her cocoon and made attempts to communicate. We appointed her as a staff in the center, and now she receives a salary which helps her support her family.

However, Lazish continues to be silent most of the time and speaks only when spoken to. It is a deafening silence at times and no amount of encouragement can make her speak. "It will take time," I tell the coordinator who gets exasperated at times.

In a country where girls and women are tutored from their childhood to remain silent, it is not easy for a girl to find her voice. Inferiority complex is inculcated in girl children from infancy; so much so that they start despising themselves and actually believing that they deserve only the worst. Thinking for themselves and voicing their own opinions is a luxury denied to millions of women in India where illiteracy and superstition reign supreme; even religious institutions take undue advantage of this social inequality.

Recently, Lazish got married. We gifted her a sewing machine instead of cash. Her husband and in-laws were obviously very happy with her. Lazish has now opened a tailoring shop in her house and is doing good business. This has boosted her confidence immensely. The girl, who was once so shy that she could not even open her mouth before the microphone, now boldly encourages other girls in her neighborhood to equip themselves with income-generating skills. Lazish is bringing about a silent revolution in the lives of underprivileged girls by teaching them to respect themselves and to speak up boldly.

## PAIN

Pain humbles the proud. It softens the stubborn. It melts the hard. Silently and relentlessly, it wins battles deep within the lonely soul. The heart alone knows its own sorrow, and not another person can fully share in it. Pain operates alone; it needs no assistance. It communicates its own message whether to statesman or servant, preacher or prodigal, mother or child. By staying, it refused to be ignored. By hurting, it reduces its victim to profound depths of anguish. And it is at that anguishing point the sufferer either submits and learns, developing maturity and character; or resists and becomes embittered, swamped by self-pity, smothered by self-will.

I have tired and I cannot find, either in Scripture or in History, a strong willed individual whom God used greatly until He allowed him/her to be hurt deeply.

*Pastor Charles R. Swindoll in " Come before winter and Share my Hope"*

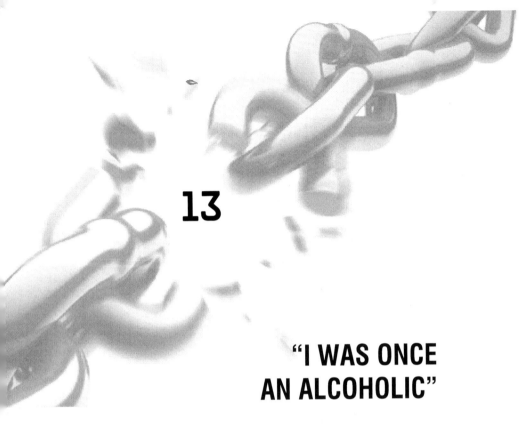

# 13

## "I WAS ONCE AN ALCOHOLIC"

*Jesus is a friend who walks in when the world has walked out.*

**I woke up** with a splitting headache. As I rubbed my eyes, the picture of the night before came alive in my mind. I had come home drunk again. At least I had managed to stagger back home.

Many times, I would fall into a ditch or by the road side. In the initial years, my family would come looking for me. But as time passed they became immune, as alcoholic had made me a slave.

It had started as a "once in a while" habit. I do not know exactly how or when it got such a tight grip on me, that I lost control of my life.

I had become a full-fledged addict and shameless too.

To get rid of the hangover, I would look for another bottle till I found myself drinking around the clock.

The village drunkard is the name I earned for myself over the years. It was normal for me to be found lying around drunk by the roadside or in the field somewhere, to be brought back by some family member.

I would often get into a brawl or get beaten. People avoided me and my family was ashamed of me. My wife who was very patient with me, finally gave up and left me taking my two children with her. I had a lot of pain in my life which I drowned in alcohol. Nobody understood me. I was hooked and as much as I tried, I could not free myself.

It had been a regular morning. I had woken up nursing a headache. I looked out of my house at the rising sun. It was still early. The household was asleep. I reached out for the radio and turned it on, hoping some music would assuage my headache.

A song about Jesus was playing. I immediately began to change the channel, wondering why on earth did I put on a Christian channel but something stopped me and I listened to the whole song. Tears began to flow as I heard the whole song.

Right at that time, Jesus spoke to me asking me to stop drinking. I was shocked.

Was I drunk? Was I dreaming?

Maybe my imagination was playing tricks with me.

After all, these many years of drinking must have definitely damaged my brain.

I cried the whole day. I remained shut inside my house that day. This was definitely not me!

I just knew that the male voice who spoke to me was Jesus'.

I do not know what came over me but I became sober. From that day onwards, I did not take a drop of alcohol.

I began to see clearly all the places where alcohol had taken me, all the roadsides, ditches, I left alcohol and am a regular listener of your program. For many days, I have been thinking of calling the phone number aired at the end of the program.

My family and the whole village is amazed by my sudden and total transformation. Many people from the neighbouring villages come to meet me to find out what resulted in such a transformation in my life. I tell them my story and about the radio broadcast.

We all believe that Jesus alone is God and has the power to transform a person's life inside out.

Many times, I think of the day when I first heard your program. What if I had changed the channel? I would have never found Jesus. My life would never have changed.

# 14

# FROM DEAD-END TO NEW HOPE

*Sometimes God calms the storm; sometimes*
*He lets the storm rage and calms His child.*

**I had reached** a dead-end. There was no way forward. I grabbed the sharp blade in my right hand and positioned it on my left wrist. I would spill all my blood, and end my pathetic life forever.

I looked around quickly with hot tears welling up in my eyes and blurring my vision. There was no one in the room. My three children were playing outside in the street. They were so very young—my heart just broke at the thought of leaving them as orphans. The children were totally oblivious of the inner turmoil I was grappling with. But I had no one to blame except myself. I was determined to end my life but as soon as I picked up the blade, I overheard a woman's voice coming from my neighbour's radio:

"Women, never consider yourselves weak. You have the power to influence and shape generations. Do not be discouraged with your problems but face them head-on. God is with you. You are not alone. Call us now if you feel discouraged and helpless."

I was stunned to hear those words. It seemed like she was speaking to me. I threw away the blade, and with tears streaming down my face, I noted down the telephone number given at the end of the program. I mustered enough courage and called up that number. In between big sobs and with tears streaming down my cheeks, I unloaded the whole truth to the counselor who had answered my call:

"I had it all," I said. "I had a loving husband, three precious children, and caring relatives and friends. In my circles, my life was the envy of many. My husband had a steady income, and I was deeply loved by him, my children, and my in-laws. My life was a dream that had come true.

"My cousin Atul often came to visit us. Atul was single, a couple of years younger than me and lived alone in a nearby city. As he lived away from his parents, he would drop in over the weekends to enjoy some homemade food. My in-laws warmly welcomed him and gave him all the respect due to a brother of the daughter-in-law of the house.

"Atul enjoyed playing with our children. He would watch me prepare food, which he thoroughly enjoyed. As time passed, he began visiting us during weekdays too. One day, in my husband's absence and when the children were sleeping soundly after returning from school, he accosted me and said, 'For many years I have been wanting to tell you that I love you. I can no longer hide my feelings for you.'

"I was shocked to hear Atul's words. 'Are you crazy?' I asked. 'I am your sister. What are you saying?'

'I know you are my cousin, but I cannot help it. I have loved you for years. It was unthinkable earlier but now I have a job. You could come away with me now,' he retorted.

"I shook my head in disbelief, still hoping that in his typical style, he would suddenly burst into laughter and say, 'I am just joking.' But he didn't.

"That day, he left quietly. For many weeks, he did not come to visit us. One day, he suddenly turned up in my husband's presence. I recall feeling very awkward and conscious. I could not even confide in anyone. How could I tell anyone that I, a married woman and a mother of three children, had a close cousin as a secret admirer? It was unthinkable for me and would bring me much shame so I kept the matter to myself.

"My cousin continued to come into our home from time to time. My family showered him with love, affection, and respect, but all along he was looking for an opportunity to catch me alone. With the passage of time, my approach toward my cousin began to soften. My husband had become very busy. His growing business was keeping him away from home for longer hours, and I missed him and those days of togetherness we used to have earlier. The children kept me on my toes, and I had no time for myself.

"Although Atul's admiration for me made me self-conscious, I started looking forward to his visits. I do not know when and how, but slowly, I too began to look for opportunities to speak to him alone. We soon became like teenagers in love. Our affair was fuelled by the private time we got with each other every afternoon as the kids slept and my mother-in-law sat under a tree gossiping with the neighbouring women and my husband was away at work. It was almost like something had taken possession of us. We could not think clearly. We were madly in love, or so I thought. I should have been wiser.

"As time passed, we desired more and more time together. Separations became unbearable. Finally, a time came when Atul asked me to choose between my husband and him. It was not so simple for me. I made it very clear to him that I would never leave my children, but surprisingly, he was ready to accept my three children also. I fell for it.

"I left my husband and home with my children to start a new life with Atul. Not once did I consider the consequences of this action on my husband and his parents. I was blindly and selfishly in love.

"The first six months with Atul were very happy. Atul looked after us very well, but as time passed, the responsibilities and expenses related to three growing children began to sour our relationship, and our love for each other began to wear thin. Finally, the day that I dreaded most came.

"Atul asked me to leave his house. He said he had made a blunder by marrying me. I was devastated. I had left my all for this man, who now wanted to get rid of me. Ashamed, embarrassed, and having no other option, I returned to my husband and his parents, who refused to even let me into the house. I tried going to my own parents, but they too were ashamed of me and would not help me. Nobody had pity even on my children. I begged them not to punish my children for my sins, but to no avail.

"I managed to stay with one of my relatives who was unaware of what I had done. She let me stay because she thought I was visiting her for some days. It was here that I decided to end my life. I knew I had reached a dead-end. My death was the only way my husband would take back my children."

It was afternoon and my relatives had gone for work. My tears were exhausted and the despair of my betrayal gnawed at my heart.

I looked around.

My children were playing quietly outside, under the shade of the big banyan tree. The radio in the neighbour's room was playing some Bollywood songs.

I took out a blade and closed my eyes which let out a volley of fresh tears. I mustered all my courage and was about to slash my wrist when suddenly, I heard a female voice speaking from the neighbour's radio saying "You are not weak. You are a woman with immense courage and power to influence generations. Never undermine yourself and never think of yourself as weak. Call us if you wish to talk to us. We are here to help and you are not alone."

I could not believe my ears. It was like someone was addressing me; someone who knew my innermost thoughts and someone who cared.

And then a soothing music played after which a telephone number was given of which I made a mental note.

I sensed some hope and very hesitantly, called the number.

A female voice responded. I shared my pain as she heard my story. It was so much easier to talk to her. She was not judgemental but listened as I wept and told her my story from the beginning to the end.

Patiently and gently, the counselor asked me to approach a local women's network that could assist me. She added, "It's alright. Now that you have realized your mistake, God will help you, but do not even think of ending your life. God is the author of life and death, and you have the responsibility of your children. Do not punish them for your sins. They need a mother."

I threw away the blade, wiped my tears, washed my face, and called out to my children. I hugged them and promised myself never again to contemplate committing suicide.

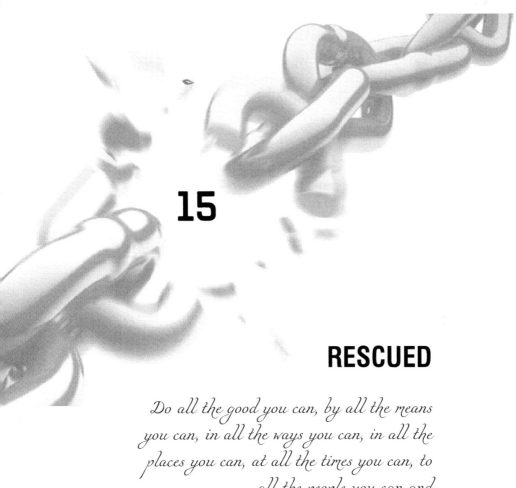

# 15

## RESCUED

*Do all the good you can, by all the means you can, in all the ways you can, in all the places you can, at all the times you can, to all the people you can and as long as you can.*

-JOHN WESLEY

**Mithu was a** 12 year old girl and lived with her father on the Indo-Bangladesh border. Her mother had died while giving birth to her. She was brought up in poverty. Many children in her village who went hungry for days. She was one of them.

Her father, a weak man with a bent back, tilled a small piece of land and they ate as and when they got some fresh produce from the landlord.

One day, her father decided to leave the village. "We will take the bus and go to Kolkata. It is a big city. I have some money saved and I will pull hand rickshaws there. We will be better placed there. Here we may die of hunger", he said.

Although Mithu had many questions, she did not ask any. She was leaving behind all her childhood memories and friends but this was a matter of filling one's stomach.

It was a hot sultry day when they arrived in Kolkata. She clung to her father's hand tenaciously. She was afraid of getting lost in this big city where buses and trams plied. The city was bustling with people. She looked at her father. He was equally nervous. Thankfully, the people spoke Bengali. Many people were sleeping on the roadside. After having some food, they slept on the pavement. After a couple of days, her father rented a hand-rickshaw. It was hard work and he did not know where to leave Mithu. The family that slept on the pavement next to them was kind. The woman had a round homely face and she took Mithu under her wings like a mother hen. She had a brood of little children whom Mithu helped in minding, lest they scurry towards a moving bus on the road. They had boiled rice for all meals. The heat, the noise and the poverty were unbearable, yet there were so many girls like Mithu around. A few months passed, when Mithu's father brought a friend along with him. "Mithu, this man will get you a job. Then we can live in a small rented room. Now you are grown up. It is good to help your *Baba*."

Mithu looked at the man. Then she looked at the father. Did she have a choice? She silently nodded.

Mithu was taken to the largest brothel in Kolkata. It was the beginning of a nightmare. When she had a moment to herself, she dreamt of the carefree life she had in the village. Sure, she did not have two square meals a day but at least she was not treated like an animal day in and day out. Mithu had nowhere to go. She had no mother, no sister and now no father as well.

After many weeks of crying and yelling, Mithu reconciled to her fate. Every day, she would be made to deck up and stand out to attract customers. Scrawny with a dark skin and layers of make-up on her face made her appear as a little girl who was trying on her mother's make up.

As her body filled, she was taught all the tricks of the trade. She had no skills, no education and this was the best she could do to earn a living.

There were many other girls in the brothel. Some her age, others older. "You will get used to it. Where else will you get the food you get here. This is easy work compared to the world outside", she was told.

But Mithu never got used to it. She cried her heart out for months till one day, she heard a radio program in Bengali. It was a story of a girl just like herself who had been brought from a village and sold off. Mithu made a note of the telephone number given at the end of the program.

She heard it again the next week and called up. She told the counselor her predicament and quickly kept the phone down.

She was frightened because she had seen girls being who tried to flee, beaten up, mercilessly.

Soon after, a man began to visit her. What she found unusual about him was that he would spend time with her but never touch her. He would sit and talk to her. This peculiar behaviour she failed to understand. He would also pay her for the time he spent with her. He would tell her about someone called Jesus who had the power to free her from this slavery.

He would come once in a while and each time Mithu was grief-stricken, she would look forward to his coming. Since the *madam* knew him as a frequent visitor, when he sought her permission to take Mithu for an outing, she agreed.

Mithu was excited.

"Bring her back tomorrow morning", yelled the *madam* as the man took Mithu away in a rickshaw.

Mithu was taken to a house where she was hidden for months. She lived with an old woman there. The old woman looked after Mithu like a daughter. In exchange, Mithu did the household chores. One day her rescuer came again. This time with a young man. He got both of them married and settled them in another city.

All of eighteen years, Mithu is now happily married to a good man.

"And where is the man who rescued you Mithu?" we ask.

"Must be busy rescuing some other girl from the brothel", Mithu responds grinning from ear to ear.

Mithu has made it her business to teach the skill of making plates using leaves to the girls and women in her neighbourhood, so they do not suffer the way she did. She also told her story for the radio so families can teach their daughters some life skills.

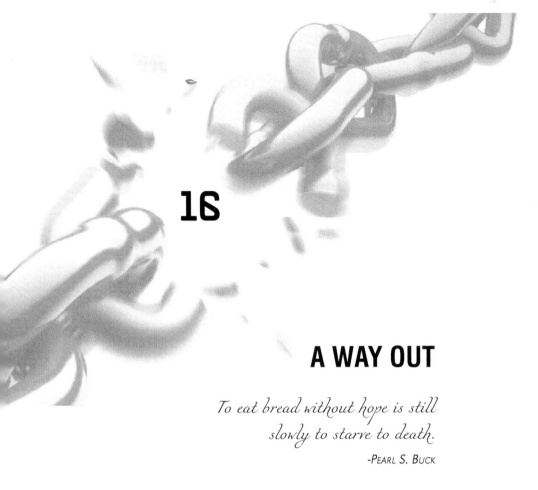

# 16

# A WAY OUT

*To eat bread without hope is still
slowly to starve to death.*

-PEARL S. BUCK

**It was stifling** hot. The radio was blaring as the workers from the adjacent factory came in for tea and snacks to the little city tea shop where I worked. Bollywood music was something that I usually enjoyed, but I was very worked up that day. I did not know with whom to share my problem. My employer kept us on our toes and his choicest expletives served like whiplashes on our dreary souls. I was terribly depressed but had no time to weep.

89

It was 4 pm. This was when a short news bulletin was being broadcast. I liked to listen to the radio; it offered information as well as entertainment. Suddenly, a woman speaker on the radio broadcast began to talk about the consequences of abortion in the context of the killing of the girl child in the womb, incidents of which were increasingly coming to light.

"What is this?" I wondered. It was as if someone was reading my innermost thoughts and my mind. I had been struggling with the thoughts of abortion but being an eighteen-year-old illiterate boy, I didn't know where to go for help.

This is my story.

We had no one but each other. We were displaced orphans born in a remote village in Bihar. Having lost our parents to hunger and sickness, my sister and I both migrated to another city to find a better life for ourselves and to escape the wrath of our extended family, who often looked for ways to torture us.

Our parents were casual farm hands. We used to till other people's lands. We had a little shack. Things were never good, but at least we had our parents with us then. One day, my father developed fever and died suddenly. We were still mourning the loss of our father, when our mother also caught the fever and died within a few days. The family members and fellow villagers began to curse us and do all kinds of black magic on us until one day we both made good our escape.

We took a bus that used to come by our village every noon; the farmers usually took their farm produce to the big city in this bus. Whatever little money we had, we planned to use it to begin a new life. Initially, I wanted to go alone, but my elder sister insisted that she wanted to accompany me. "I will also find some work in the big city, and we can make a fresh start. I do not wish to lose you after losing our parents," she said. Her words made sense to me. She was right—we had only each other.

The city was big and crowded. We rented a tiny room to live in. Things were way more expensive here than what we had expected. There were lots of people in the city. We often stood and stared in bewilderment at the big shops, cars, and massive trucks, and it took some time to get used to this new way of life.

Most of the people were educated and went to school or to work. We both did not have any skills other than our ability to do manual labour. After being driven from pillar to post, I managed to get a job in a small shop. I was underpaid, but at least, I had a job. Once I learned the ropes and gained some experience, I could try for a better job in the future.

While I worked in the shop, my sister stayed alone in our tiny rented room. Every morning, she would pack some bread for me, which I would carry with me for lunch. Sometimes, we would have some vegetable curry, and at other times, some boiled rice. We both looked starved and miserable but had to make do with what we had.

Not only were we sad but also unhappy and angry at the way our life was turning out to be. We were young and had dreams. At least, dreams did not cost money. We were glad that we could just let our imagination run loose and sleep soundly every night.

Days turned into months and soon my sister voiced her desire to pick up a job too. But who would give her a job? I was aware that she was growing up and needed to be married. I was also aware that men used to stare at her and pass lewd remarks. Being a girl and moreover, economically deprived made her all the more vulnerable. But I could not do anything because the meagre money that I brought home was barely enough to keep our stomachs full. Besides, I was also putting aside some pennies for a rainy day.

My employer was a kind man when he was relaxed. That was one bright spot in my life. He taught me the work, gave us two cups of tea during the day, and kept the radio blaring as we worked. Not only did we have information about what was happening in the world, but we also we had entertainment in the form of songs. He also used to keep the shop closed one day in a week, and this was when my sister and I would go about in the big city and look around. We often envied people who could splurge on food and clothes that we could never dream of purchasing. My sister usually got frustrated after such outings and would often talk to me about other jobs that were available to girls her age, but I did not pay much attention to her concerns. I ignored her because there was little I could do to assuage her bitterness. I could understand that like any other girl, she dreamt of marrying and having a family of her own but here she was stuck with her younger brother. I too felt very responsible for her but could not do anything for her marriage.

And then, one day I got a shock. It was a hot summer day. The humidity in the atmosphere had given me a headache, and I requested for short leave to go home and rest. My kind employer let me go because there was not much work that day. But when I reached home, I was not prepared for what I saw. In our tiny room, there was a man with my sister; they too were not expecting me home so early. They were shocked and shaken. I was very angry with my sister.

I was so mad at my sister that I wanted to kill her. I recognized the man. I had seen him around and even caught both of them exchanging glances a few times, but I had been too preoccupied with other pressing matters. I had not quite taken the matter seriously. I sent the man away. Next day onward, I started locking up my sister in the tiny room when I went to work.

Time passed, and soon the monsoons arrived. Our tiny room became more and more unbearable to live in. As water leaked in through the roof, we stayed close to each other. One night, to my shock, my sister seduced me. I had not known a woman before. I did not know how to react, but I must confess, I did not resist her too much either. I knew what we were doing was wrong. She was my sister, but we

94

had unfulfilled desires. This way no one would suspect us. To the neighbours, we were just siblings.

But I was very unhappy and felt guilty. One night, when I came home, she informed me that she was with child. She also said that she would never marry or go to another man but always live with me. I was deeply troubled. I had nowhere to turn to. We were young orphans trying to save ourselves from the big bad world, but now we were in a quagmire.

I began to wallow in self-pity and went into depression. I thought of getting drunk but later decided against it. Now, I would have another mouth to feed; I certainly was in no position to take on additional responsibilities. I had to find some solution. I decided to take my sister to one of the abortion clinics in the big city and get rid of the child.

I had it all lined up very well. I would borrow some money from my employer and take my sister to one of the abortion clinics. But I was jolted out of my thoughts on hearing the radio broadcast—the Bollywood songs gave way to an anchor's voice mentioning the ill-effects of abortion. I was aghast. She mentioned cancer, infertility, mental retardation, and suicidal tendencies as the repercussions of aborting a child. A phone number was also given. I called up the number and spoke to the counselor but did not have the courage to tell her about my sister's pregnancy.

The kind voice on the other side gave me the courage to open up, and slowly I began to call daily and ask for help. I began to feel relieved. The counselor was not judgmental but was very kind and wanted to help me. Over time, I divulged all the details of my physical relationship with my sister. The counselor seemed a little shocked initially. She stated that a brother–sister relationship is very highly esteemed in our culture, and this relationship should never be misused. I agreed that we had made a mistake. We felt guilty but did not know what to do. She guided me to get my sister married and to stop my incestuous relationship with my sister right away.

I accepted her guidance and started searching for a boy. After one month, I found a suitable boy who was ready to marry my sister if I paid him Rs. 10,000/-. With great difficulty, I took a loan from several people and got my sister married. Now my sister is happily married and lives in the village with her husband and child.

I cannot imagine what would have happened if I had not heard the radio broadcast and received wise counsel. Perhaps my sister and I would have committed suicide. Who knows?

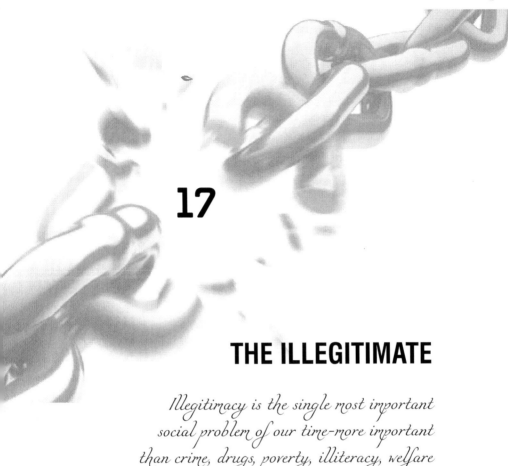

# 17

# THE ILLEGITIMATE

*Illegitimacy is the single most important social problem of our time-more important than crime, drugs, poverty, illiteracy, welfare or homelessness, because it drives everything else."*

**A 12 year** old boy spoke into the phone, hesitantly and fearfully,

"Hello, my name is Rahul and I just heard your radio broadcast."

"Hello Rahul, how are you? Thank you for calling in."

"Ma'am, I heard you say in your program that God considers all human life precious and He loves us. Do you think He would love me? Everyone in my village hates me because I am an illegitimate child of my mother."

"No Rahul, God loves you. He ordained for you to be born into this world. You are a unique creation of God."

This was the first conversation that Rahul had with our counselor but not the last. It has been a year since he first called and now practically every month he calls in and gives us updates about himself.

This is Rahul's story in his own words.

Being hated, slighted, ridiculed and rejected has been my portion since I came to my senses. My first childhood memories of love shown was only by my mother. My extended family, the neighbours and my fellow villagers have always cursed me.

I was told that my father had impregnated my mother and abandoned her. My mother chose to give me birth in spite of all the social stigma. She is raising me single-handedly with the meagre salary she receives from the local school where she works as a maid.

I used to wander away alone, awkward and trying to stay away from people as much as I could.

I hated going to school too because even there I was met with the same behavior. I did not feel like studying or playing with other children. I was like a social outcaste.

I often wondered, "Is it my fault that I was born out of wedlock? Is an innocent child illegitimate or is the sexual union of two consenting adults outside of marriage illegitimate? What did I do to deserve society's wrath?"

Only deafening silence was my portion.

My little transistor was my best friend. I listened to it after returning from school. I enjoyed a variety of programs including the songs. It's interesting that in our country, there is a song on every subject.

One day, as I was sitting by myself, I heard a radio program that was encouraging girls to have self-respect and not despise themselves just because the society disrespects them. Although the program was targeted towards girls' empowerment, I thought to myself, "I am a boy and yet, people despise me. I should not listen to people. I need to be strong from inside."

I immediately noted down the telephone number and called up. A friendly and warm voice responded. I was hesitant but then I told her my life story. Somehow, I felt safe trusting her with this truth.

The counselor encouraged me and told me things I had never heard before. She said that my mother could have aborted me but my mother loves me and I should not despise myself because God brought me into this world and He has great plans for me.

I was very encouraged by her words.

I continue to listen to your radio programs and have promised to myself that I will study well and get all the respect for my mother which my father and society did not give.

# 18

# MY GIRLFRIEND IS PREGNANT!

*Discouraged people don't need critics. They hurt enough already. They don't need more guilt or piled-on distress. They need Encouragement. They need a refuge: willing, caring and available.*

–PASTOR CHARLES R. SWINDOLL

**"Hello, my name** is Gaurav, and I am calling after listening to your program on abortion," a small voice fearfully hissed into the telephone of our radio counselor.

"I am very scared," he whispered into the phone. Our counselor's gentle voice encouraged him to continue speaking while she assured him that she was listening.

"I am a student, and I got involved with a girl in my class. Now she is pregnant. We wanted to get an abortion, but we heard your radio broadcast and are now scared of the abortion. We want help! There is nobody here whom we can trust. Is it true...what we heard on radio ...that abortion is dangerous for the mother?"

"Do you want to tell me in detail about what happened so that I can help you accordingly?" persisted our counselor.

This is what Gaurav shared.

"Pooja and I study in the same college. Her brother and I are friends. We grew up together. Pooja and I began to get conscious of each other only recently. I began to notice that she wore her hair quite long, and she looked at me coyly from below her long eyelashes. She was no longer the little girl who used to prance around with a running nose and untidy pigtails.

At some point, we do not know when, our friendship blossomed into love. At the back of our minds, we knew our relationship would never have the approval of our families—for one, we belonged to different castes. Our marriage was unthinkable.

Secondly, we were still students and financially dependent. Our parents had invested in us. Pooja's family, especially, had bypassed the social taboo associated with sending girls to school—that too, a co-educational school. But we had become blind to everything. My dream of moving to Delhi to start a business and Pooja's dream of becoming a teacher were all forgotten. We could only think of each other all day long.

We began seeking solitude and would saunter off, holding hands, into the nearby forest area with a small transistor. We would lie under big shady trees and watch the cattle graze and idly look at us as we listened to romantic Bollywood songs, which further fuelled our love and emotions for each other.

The birds would sing happily and the frogs in the nearby pond would jump in and out, making us giggle. It was so nice to be this close to nature and to each other. The result of our closeness was that our friends began to miss us, and they started asking us questions. Soon our grades started falling. Although we made efforts to study, we could only see each other's face in our textbooks. We wrote each other's name in the notebooks. We day dreamed about each other.

But the worst outcome of our intimacy came to light when Pooja announced, 'I am pregnant.' We were both horrified! We could not believe what had happened. We loved each other deeply; yet the fear of social stigma and the loss of family honour petrified us.

We did not know where to turn. We were both helpless and fearful. We even contemplated suicide. We did not know whom to trust and where to go for help because word would leak out, and we would be deep trouble with our families.

In this state of mind, while both of us were sitting in our favorite hideout in the forest, we heard a radio program.

Oddly, amidst the film songs, the radio program was also giving information about the effects of abortion on a woman's body. The more we heard the speaker, the more fearful we became. The speaker explained how abortion could lead to cancer, infertility, and the birth of retarded children and cause adverse emotional and psychological effects.

I love Pooja and cannot think of these terrible consequences happening to her, so I quickly noted down the telephone numbers given at the end of the program and called in. Is what Madam said on the program true?"

The gentle voice at the other end of the phone said, "Yes, whatever you heard is true. But do not worry. Just go and talk to your parents. You are still very young. You have made a mistake, but your parents will forgive you. They will guide you. Moreover, the baby is made in the image of God. Aborting the baby would be equivalent to murder, which is a sin."

Gaurav was terrified of sharing the truth with his parents. He said, "What if our parents get us both killed? Maybe both of us should run away from home, but I have no money or skills for a job and no place to stay."

Sleepless nights followed for both of them.

Gaurav was more concerned about Pooja because her family honour was at stake. He voiced his concerns to the radio counselor who continued encouraging him to speak to his parents.

However, Gaurav was afraid. As time passed, he became concerned that Pooja's pregnancy would become evident; the baby bump would begin to show!

Gaurav called the counselor daily, and every day she encouraged him to share the truth with his parents. She gave them a lot of support. Gaurav found it easy to share with the counselor since he was confiding in a total stranger; also, she was kind and far from being judgmental.

Finally, Gaurav summoned all his courage and shared with his parents. Initially, they were very angry. They were concerned about their studies and their careers. But finally, they relented and went to meet Pooja's parents. Gaurav and Pooja were quickly married in a simple ceremony. The couple is currently living with Gaurav's parents; they are expecting their baby soon.

Gaurav called in one last time to say that they were very happy and grateful to the counselor for showing them the right direction when they needed it the most.

# 19

## LITTLE KNOWN

*If you think education is expensive,*
*try ignorance.*

*- DEREK BOK*

**We are first** cousins and we grew up in a joint family in a very congested area of old Delhi. In our culture, women are covered from head to toe, in a black outfit, be it summer, winter or rain. Many a times, I notice that when my married cousins would go out with their husbands, they hurriedly remove their thick black gowns as soon as they became out of sight from the prying eyes of the family elders.

107

I have often observed the envious looks my sisters give to the women in the market place as they showed off their colourful clothes, hair bands and make up.

The women in our family also wear make-up and henna but only at home, within the women groups and their own husbands. Outside in the street, only their eyes are visible.

I feel bad for the women in my family but can do or say little. They have reconciled to their fate but there is one cousin who name is Shabana. She is barely eighteen and is my first cousin and is very unhappy with her lot.

Day in and day out, she shares her frustration with me. We became friends when we were children.. In the midst of so many cousins and elders, we were always found to be together. Be it sitting on Abba's two wheeler as it stood outside our old sprawling ancestral house or playing for hours at a stretch, we were always together. We enjoyed each other's company. Our other cousins were also our friends but both of us had a special bonding.

"Let's get them married when they are older," our mothers would often laugh and look at us as we, not understanding anything, would run off hand in hand.

I used to go to school but not Shabana. This frustrated her. So I began sharing everything I learnt at school with her. We used to sit on the terrace behind the water tanks, away from prying eyes and noise.

I used to teach her everything I learnt at school. As time passed and we entered into puberty, I noticed Shabana had begun to change. She was no longer the little girl with pigtails. She was an excellent cook and was trained well in all household chores and at the age of fourteen her Abba was already looking for a good match for her.

"But your mom wanted us to get married," I teased and she would run around the water tank as I chased her, saying, "First grow up and get a job. Who will give his daughter to you when you are not even earning yet?"

And we would laugh.

I do not remember the exact moment I fell in love with her.

Was it at our cousin's wedding when we travelled in the night bus accompanied by our entire clan and she sat with me and slept with her head on my shoulder, as the radio played soft romantic songs from Bollywood, or was it when she wore a red flowing dress at a family gathering with henna on her lustrous hair giving it a burgundy shade. I do not remember. But I do remember how much I adored the bright tones of henna designs on her petite feet and palms as our cousins teased her saying, "The darker the henna, the more your husband will love you." Looking coyly in my direction, she fled from the scene.

By then, I knew that even Shabana had feelings for me. She would avoid me and give me coy looks and giggle and hide behind other cousins.

It was a moonlit night. I was studying by a small bulb for my exam and Shabana came and sat beside me. The cool breeze made us both shudder. It was either the breeze or the intense emotions we felt for each other. Whatever it was, that night was one I will remember for as long as I live.

The same ritual followed night after night and nobody was any wiser, till one day I heard these words fall on me like a bomb, " I think I am pregnant. I've been missing my periods for the past two months. My parents are going to kill me."

I was scared out of my wits. But as the initial shock wore off, I began to think of ways to get rid of the pregnancy. We could not hide it for long, even in the black shroud that Shabana wore. I had to move fast.

So one day on the pretext of taking her to her friend's house, I took her to an abortion clinic. There were many around and it was easy. I had done my home work and I took her to one that was very far from our place. No names would be asked, it would be quick and Shabana would be back home by evening. In the form we ticked on the category of major. We had no choice. Sure enough, it was easy. Thanks to the money I had stolen from my father's purse. With such a huge family, he was kept guessing as to who would have done it and I got away. My mother made it easier for me when she reminded him, " When you came home drunk the other night, you must have dropped the money and not realised."

No one doubted me. I had anyway, never stolen money before.

One night, as I lay on the terrace, alone, looking at the stars, I mused. " Did we do the right thing? Our religion does not permit us to kill the unborn child. But what choice did we have?"

In an effort to change my mood, I put on the small radio which sat beside me. With the family fighting over channels, I preferred to be alone with my radio as it offered me entertainment and information. Shabana had been very upset. She had cried all the way—to and from the abortion clinic—I was upset too but what could we do?

It was best that she be left alone for a couple of days.

" You are listening to a special broadcast on abortion", declared the announcer. "What on earth?" I sat upright. Here I was trying to take my mind off abortion and listen to some music and here they were talking about abortion.

I had never heard about abortion before, atleast not on the radio. I increased the volume and heard the whole talk. I was not prepared for what I heard. Without realising, I had pushed Shabana into a very dangerous zone. The voice on the radio explained the risks of abortion and how God intended the womb to protect the child but how humans turn it into a tomb. It continued further to say, "Mother Teresa said, 'If a child is not safe in his or her mother's womb, where in the world will he or she be safe?' The consequences of abortion are breast cancer, infertility and birth of retarded children. It also leads to depression and increases risk of suicide."

By the time the program finished, I was weeping like a baby. I loved Shabana. How could I have done this to her? I called up the phone number given at the end of the broadcast and hesitantly, after changing my name said, "I did not know all this about abortion. I have just got an abortion done for the girl I love. What should I do now?

Can I still marry her? I am afraid. What if she cannot have children any more or what if she commits suicide?"

The voice on the other side of the phone was gentle and re-assuring. The counselor consoled me and advised me to not abandon Shabana, but to marry her soon.

"How I wished you had broadcast this program earlier. I would never have killed our unborn child", I said remorsefully. I decided to quit my studies, make a man of myself by getting a job and ask her *Abba* for her hand in marriage.

# 20

# UNSAFE HAVEN

*People don't care how much you know, until they know how much you care....about them.*

- ZIG ZIGLAR

**"My alcoholic brother** is attempting to rape me. My paralysed mother and I are helpless. Please help me sell my kidney through your radio broadcast or I will throw myself in front of a moving truck" were the words stuttered out of a young girl named Antra's mouth while she spoke to the phone counselor.

Since it was a frantic call for help from the city where I lived, went to meet her. As the driver took me through the crowded, filthy and lanes, he muttered, "Madam, where have you brought me?" As he pulled the tyres out of a mud pit, his white cab splashed mud.

The lanes intertwined with one another for almost an hour before I finally reached my destination.

Barely 18, (as she told me later ) but looking 13 due to poor health, she lived in a two room dingy house with her paralysed mother. Even the alcoholic brother lived with his skinny wife who carried a two year old in her lap while the older one hung shyly to her grubby dress. A baby bump showed that she was expecting the third child any time soon.

We sat under a tree and Antra told me her story.

"I have an elder sister who is married. My mother became paralysed due to a nerve injury caused by a negligent doctor during a surgery. My alcoholic brother does not work, beats us up, including his wife and is forcing us to sell this house which is our only shelter. I am a tailor by profession and can tailor clothes for a living but I do not have a sewing machine. I heard your program on women empowerment but never thought that you would come to meet me yourself. I always thought radio people do not relate to ordinary masses."

From then began our journey with Antra.

We first provided her with a sewing machine with which she began to make a living. With the passage of time, we appointed her as a tailoring teacher to one of our projects and she began to gain confidence to move in public transport, talk to people and become financially independent.

It was good to see Antra blossom into a responsible young lady.

Time continued to pass and she kept in touch.

One Saturday morning, Antra's name flashed in my mind and I called her up happily surprising her. She told me about a man she had met in the market a couple of days ago, who had invited her home. He said that he was in the business of training young girls like her make jewellery. He also said that he had a wife at home and together they trained the girls. Needy as she still was, Antra had planned on going.

I immediately cautioned her. The area where she lived was the hub of flesh trade. She pondered upon my advice and decided against going.

After a passage of time, we appointed her as a tailoring teacher with our hostel girls. Meanwhile, her mother passed away. So Antra went to live with her elder sister. Time passed and she got a job in a car factory where she was trained to assemble automobile parts.

When a marriage proposal came for her, she checked with me and her elder sister. With all found to be well, the marriage alliance was sealed.

Now she is happily married and lives in a town near Delhi. With her mother-in-law's help, she has opened her own tailoring shop and is doing a good business and is a confident businesswoman today.

She continues to listen to our radio broadcasts and encourages people to listen to them too.

Her words during a radio interview continue to ring in my ears, "*Had it not been for the radio broadcast I accidentally heard that melancholic evening, I would have committed suicide.*"

# 21

# HOPE CONCEIVED

*No one is useless in this world who lightens*
*the burden of it to anyone else.*

-CHARLES DICKENS

**Aloka was an** escapist by nature. She left her village as a
young teenager with the first boy who made a pass at her.

Her father had died and her mother wanted to marry
her to an old man in exchange for some money. She had
overheard it all when her maternal uncle had come to visit
her recently widowed mother. They both thought she was
asleep in the small corner of their dark and dingy hut. She
had been asleep but the sound of hushed conversation
accompanied by the sound of big raindrops falling noisily

to the ground had woken her up. She had been very tired. The heat and humidity typical of the little village close to the Bay of Bengal was awful. The rain was a welcome sign and she changed side on her untidy little floor bed and kept her eyes closed and quietly overheard their conversation.

"How will you take care of her. Look at her. She is growing up and soon she will attract a beeline of men. You are better off if you marry her to the old man. She will be safe and you too will have money for your old age."

Her mother was nodded her head.

"You are right. Now with her father no more, how will we feed ourselves and her younger siblings. I know you mean well. Alright then. You do as you deem fit."

Aloka knew her fate was sealed. But she did not wish to marry. She had been watching movies and listening to the radio broadcasting romantic songs. She had dreams of her own. She did not wish to waste her life here in this impoverished little village. She wanted to see the big city.

Her mind was frantic with scheming and immediately went back to the village rogue who had been making passes at her. If anyone could get her out of this poverty-stricken village it was him.

Babu was the rebel of the village, detested by all. But he was ambitious and enterprising. She had often overheard him bragging about his escapades in the big town to the eyes-bulging and open-mouthed villagers. He would often take the bus to the city and bring back things to sell to the villagers.

For Babu every village girl was a potential target. He had often whistled at Aloka when she would return from the well balancing pots of water on her head and holding a couple of others in her hands. The evening Sun would illuminate her sultry oval face and small eyes. She was voluptuous and had dark long hair. She knew she looked good.

As the first opportunity presented itself, she approached Babu. "My family wants to marry me off against my will. Can you take me to the city? Please help me." She blurted. Babu was surprised at her boldness. They decided to leave the village the same night and never look back.

In the big city, Aloka lived with Babu for a few months but soon he began bringing his friends home to her. "I am making money for you. How else will we survive in this city. We're unemployed and don't possess any skills" he said.

He was right. Work was work. Her needs were being met and she was much better off than the girls in the brothel. Here in a small rented flat, it was just them and the clients. Life was good.

They got used to each other and this way of life. Aloka they would go to the city and explore the markets whenever she got time off.

As time passed, with good food, Aloka grew healthy and turned into a woman. She had no regrets about her life and the men who came and went meant only work until she got pregnant.

Babu knew every thing and took her to an abortion clinic. She rested for a week before she began entertaining clients again.

Time passed and she had many abortions.

She wondered why each time, she grew more and more depressed and suicidal. She wanted to quit this way of life. But Babu refused. He tried to humour her and please her in different ways, to no avail.

One day she decided that she had had enough. Once again, silently, she schemed her escape. Like her mother who had not known what was going on in her mind, Babu knew nothing about her scheme.

There was a Haryana truck driver who used to visit her often. He was a big fellow with beard and a turban. He had often asked Aloka to come away with him. "I live up north in Haryana and there are no girls in our village. I will marry you. You can escape from this place. Nobody will know. I will fix Babu....."

Until this point, Aloka had not given it a thought. But now after a number of abortions, she wanted to leave this life behind.

One day, she eloped with the Haryana driver and came to Delhi.

She could not speak a word of their language and saw their clothing and food habits were very different from what she was used to. It was a big joint family of many brothers and old women. Most of the brothers had wives from other parts of India.

Aloka tried to settle as a family woman but with the passage of time when she did not conceive, she began to get restless. Her husband began to get upset with her. He wanted children and she could give him none. She began to get bored and one day she asked him, " When you are gone for days, I get bored. There is a factory nearby. Why don't I pick up a job? I can make tea for them or cook for them. What do you say?"

Her husband agreed and he got her the job. Once again Aloka's scheming began and she began to go with the men in the factory in order to get pregnant. But she did not.

Here at her home, she was humiliated by her mother in law. The other women had borne children and they were one growing brood.

Humiliated, Aloka would break down time and again. But only when she was alone. She began to recede further into isolation. One would think that with the passage of time, the wound of her barrenness would heal. May be it left un-touched it would heal but if raked up day in and day out; the wound would ooze again. One morning, she played with the radio knob and heard a melodious song being played. It sounded like a religious program. She had never heard this one before. That was the first time she heard the name JESUS. She felt a strange peace fill her heart. She felt compelled to call the telephone number given at the end of the program.

She quickly made a note of the telephone number on a piece of paper. At the first opportunity she got, she called up the number and was warmly responded to. Hesitantly,

Aloka spoke to the counselor requesting for prayer for her to have a child.

She was encouraged to continue to listen to the radio program which she began to do on a weekly basis. She told her husband about the program and they both began to listen to the programs.

Weekly conversations with the counselor became a habit. Aloka shared everything about her personal life. The pain, the humiliation and the bitterness of it all. She was listened to. Unburdening to a stranger felt like therapy. She wanted to mend her ways. The counselor encouraged her to be faithful to her husband.

Time continued to pass.

One day the much awaited call from her came to our counselor saying, " I am pregnant. I have just come from the Doctor and after my husband you are the first one I am giving this good news to. Thank you for introducing me to Jesus. I want to come and see you. I want to meet you. God has answered my prayers."

The news of Aloka's pregnancy spread like wild fire in the village.

"Women are listening to our radio broadcast and calling up to request for counselling and prayer. "We have a big group here and all of us want to meet you. Please come and visit us."

# 22

# LONESOME

*A coincidence is a small miracle where God prefers to remain anonymous*

**I was nearing** 35 years and lonesome. The fact that I lived in a joint family was no relief because as my brothers and sisters got married and had families of their own, I felt lonelier.

I was unemployed and hence no one wanted to marry their daughter to me. I often used to wander away into the fields with my transistor in my hand. That was my only friend. Usually, I would get up in the mornings to saunter into the fields.

One day, I heard a devotional program in the morning. I listened to it very carefully as I watched the sunrise. It somehow touched a chord in my heart. Was it the songs or was it the Word that was being read out? I am not sure, but definitely there was something that kept me attracted to it. As the announcer signed off, I made a mental note of the timings of the next broadcast and I heard it again the next week and then again the next week. I began to enjoy it and used to look forward to it. The announcer's voice encouraging the listeners to call urged me to call and with great hesitation, one day I called the number.

A kind and compassionate female voice responded and thanked me for calling in. I mustered all my strength and introduced myself. I told her that I was unemployed, single and depressed, but enjoyed listening to *Satya Vachan*.

She prayed for me along with me on the phone and within a week I got a job.

My faith in Christ began to grow. I began to regularly listen to the two Christian devotional programs and requested prayer for marriage.

Soon after I got a job, I got married.

I like my wife very much. We are very happy. I shared about my faith in Christ with her. I then requested for a Bible. I wanted to read the Bible for myself after hearing portions of it on the radio, Soon my wife became pregnant but due to some medical issue, the doctor advised abortion.

Again I called up the counselor and she sent me material on *Life in the Womb*. I also heard the radio program on the consequences of abortion. We decided not to go for an abortion. Instead, we prayed.

Everything is well and my wife and baby are fine and we are all growing in the Lord Jesus. Thank you so much!

# 23

# FLIGHT TO FREEDOM

*Live to love. Love to live—*

AMY CARMICHAEL

**Kanika woke up** all excited and full of energy that day—it was Rakshabandhan, a very special day for her. Being the only sister of six bothers in a big town in India, Kanika cherished this festival that celebrated the love between a brother and a sister.

Kanika knew she was pampered because she was the youngest child in the joint family. In her village, it uncommon for girls to go to college, but she had been allowed this special privilege by her family, and had completed her Master's degree. This was possible because she had insisted that she wanted to pursue higher studies instead of getting married at an early age.

"For what purpose?" the brothers would ask her. "You have to get married some day, and your husband will look after you."

"All of you have professions. I too would like to have one," Kanika would retort as she stamped her feet in protest.

This would melt the hearts of her brothers, and they would all become very quiet. Kanika used to enjoy this power she had over her brothers. She even secretly revelled in being the envy of her sisters-in-law, who had been married young and were stuck with their household chores while she scooted off to college.

The town was afraid of her brothers. They were powerful men with strong connections and hoarse voices. But on Rakshabandhan day, their softer side surfaced. The brothers knelt before Kanika and gazed adoringly at her. After saying all the prayers, she tied large colorful *rakhis*[1] on their wrists as they gifted her cash and jewelry, blessed her, and kissed her on her forehead.

"Today, I would like to ask you for a special gift. Will you give me?" asked Kanika.

"What is it? they asked in unison. "You know we love you. You are our only precious sister. Test us."

"Will you let me marry the man of my choice?"

A stunned silence followed.

---

1 A *rakhi* is a sacred thread that a girl ties on her brother's wrist on the occasion of Rakshabandhan.

The joyful atmosphere at home suddenly became very tense. The octogenarian parents who overheard Kanika began to weep and curse. The sisters-in-law were stunned that Kanika could dare ask such a question, but Kanika's gaze was focused only on her brothers, especially her eldest brother, who was a lawyer.

The silence prolonged. "We will discuss this later," said her eldest brother.

Kanika agreed and dashed off to college. She always seemed to be in a hurry, saying she had to attend classes. But actually, she used to go to meet Atul, the love of her life; they met every morning before going to college. Atul was her senior in college; he had now started working. Before going to class, Kanika met Atul every morning before he went to work. They had fallen in love a couple of years back. It was a socially forbidden love affair because Atul belonged to a lower caste. Kanika knew of the social stigma associated with marrying a man belonging to a lower caste, but education had sensitized her to caste discriminations. She had learnt to think and live freely, and did not feel bound by the restrictions of the rigid caste system, which had enslaved people for centuries.

Atul had always been scared of the consequences of their love—but not Kanika. She was confident that her brothers would stand by her decision because they loved her to bits.

That evening, her eldest brother took Kanika aside and asked her to write a note that stated, "I am committing suicide out of my own accord because I am very unhappy with my life."

"But why?" enquired Kanika.

"Just write this and I will tell you why?" he replied.

Trusting her brother, she wrote the note, signed it, and handed it over to him.

Her brother responded calmly, "We have found out all about Atul and your relationship with him. We cannot condone it. We love you very much but remember your honour is attached to the family's honour. If you take one wrong step, I want you to know that we will kill both of you."

Kanika was stunned. Was she dreaming?

The lawyer brother's voice remained calm and patient. There was no anger, no shouting, just a cold, calculated, and pre-meditated strategy to make sure she obeyed the family's decision.

"We have found a boy for you and within a fortnight you will be married. You will no longer be meeting Atul. If you do, we will kill him. We will give you what you want. We love you, but we cannot allow you to marry outside our caste and bring a bad name to our family for generations. People will spit on us."

"But brother . . ." A startled Kanika lapsed into silence as her brother pointed his strong index finger right into her face.

She could barely believe that this was the same brother whom she loved so much; he had never before threatened her like this. Confused and speechless, Kanika returned to her room. She did not sleep the whole night. She hoped this was a nightmare that would soon end.

Everyone looked normal the next morning. Kanika gathered enough courage and went to her brother; she agreed to all that he had said.

"I will marry the man you want me to," she said. "But please allow me to go to college one last time. I have to get my certificates and enquire about my result, which is due any time now."

Relieved that the sister was obeying the decision of the family, the brother hugged her and off went Kanika. Atul was waiting for her at their usual hideout. Fearfully looking over her shoulders to ensure that she was not followed, Kanika quickly poured out her heart to him.

"Tonight, meet me at the bus stand, and we will leave this town," said Kanika.

"What are you saying?" Atul retorted.

"I cannot even think of marrying another man," she sobbed as Atul embraced her. Moreover, my brothers will kill me. They have already made me write the suicide note."

"All right. I will take the help of my friend. We need money, and I will need to gather some stuff. I have a friend in another town; we could go and stay with him for some time."

"See you tonight at the bus-stand. After 11 p.m., there are different buses every hour going into different directions, and my brothers will never find us."

Kanika got back from college early that day. The news of her marriage had been announced by her father and plans were being made for the festivities. The father explained to the various relatives: "The boy's family was waiting for Kanika to finish her studies. He is a school teacher. They are in favour of the education of girls. They are a good family. Our Kanika will be very happy. They are in our town as well, so we can visit our sister and she can visit us anytime."

The happy chatter and the relaxed family discussions continued until late into the night. Kanika had kept a relaxed countenance giving the impression that she had accepted her fate. Her brothers lovingly patted her on her head as they went to bed.

Kanika too went into her room and a couple of hours later when the household had slept, Kanika left the house for good. As she stepped out of the door, she knew she was as good as dead for her family. A wave of sadness swept over her, but the thought of living without Atul was unthinkable.

She dashed towards the bus stop where Atul was waiting for her. They boarded the night bus and sped away to a nearby town where they stayed with Atul's friend. After a week, Kanika started feeling uncomfortable. Although they enjoyed the anonymity associated with a big town and often stayed indoors, she felt insecure about not being married. As time passed, the friend too began to ask for money because he was finding it difficult to feed three people. Also, he could not continue to risk his life for their sake. If Kanika's brothers found out about Atul's friend, they would certainly get even with him.

With each passing day, Kanika's anxiety grew. She had sealed the door to her past, but the future looked hopeless. Many nights and days of crying passed, when one evening, she casually turned on the radio and heard a radio program about honor killings. She immediately called the number provided on the program and shared her story. The counselor connected her to an advocate who advised her to get married in a temple and in a court and also to file a complaint in the local police station about the suicide note that her brother had forced her to write.

Kanika followed the advice.

A few days later, she called the radio counselor to say that she and Atul were married and were now looking for jobs to sustain themselves. They also stated how grateful they were for receiving proper direction when they were absolutely alone, afraid, and hopeless.

# 24

# ARRANGED MARRIAGE

*God created marriage. No government subcommittee envisioned it. No social organization developed it. Marriage was conceived and born in the mind of God."*

– MAX LUCADO

**I woke up** to the smell of incense burning. It was rose incense today. My father was a temple Priest and it was his practice to perform rituals every morning in our home before he left for his temple duties. I was the youngest in the family. All other siblings were married and had moved out.

A cool breeze blew in through my room's window beckoning the onset of monsoons. I gazed out and saw the leaves from the top of the banyan tree in our courtyard dancing as if inviting me to come out and play with my friends. I jumped out of my bed. Today was a Sunday and my friends and I had made a plan to visit the nearby town to do some shopping. We used to walk. All of us, in a group. Sometimes, we would cycle.

We lived in a beautiful town on the banks of a river. I was very happy and content with my life. We had plenty. My mother rarely cooked as people used to bring food to our home. We could not afford the luxuries our neighbours could, nevertheless, we had a variety of cooked meals that were brought to my father to be blessed before setting before the idols.

My father was a big advocate of girls' education. Every day I used to walk down to my school with my childhood friends. Long pigtails tied with bright red ribbons and heavy school bags were the hallmark of our group. Since we belonged to the same neighbourhood, we had long conversations along the way.

We also liked to listen to the radio a lot. A couple of us had the new phone on which radio broadcasts could be heard. We listened to film music, news and had long discussions as we walked and talked for miles.

One day, one of my school friends heard a broadcast called *Disha*. "They talk about women issues and encourage all girls to get an education and become financially independent", she said encouraging us to listen to it too.

Peer pressure caused me to listen to the weekly broadcast. We used to listen and discuss every week. We heard interviews of girls and women who had suffered tragedies and had risen from misery towards a hope-filled life. Many were school girls like us. It was fun.

This became a ritual for us; to discuss the subject of the *Disha* radio program.

One day, one of my friends told us that the people who speak on *Disha* also speak on a morning devotional program. We began to listen to that broadcast too. I liked it very much. It had a very soothing scripture reading accompanied by songs which I loved to hear. Soon, we as a group began to memorise and sing those songs. One day, one of my friends called up and asked for a Bible. We knew Bible is a Holy Book and talks about God.

I personally began to grow in my faith in Jesus.

Time passed and nobody in my family knew about my love for Jesus. We already worshipped many gods and goddesses, so having another one was not an issue. I had been taught to show respect towards all religions.

What I did not realise was that as I listened regularly to the words of Jesus, I began to love Him deeply.

One day, a family came to visit us. There was nothing unusual about it except for the fact that my mother made me wear a sari and carry a tea tray for the visitors. I was suspicious because almost all the girls of my age had got married or were getting married.

I was angry. I stamped my feet and made my displeasure evident after the guests had left. "You know I want to go to college and earn a living. Why will you not permit me to study?"

However, my father would not give in. He was adamant. I called up the radio counselor and cried my heart out. I loved Jesus and would not marry a person from another faith.

Yes, there was little I could do. The counselor encouraged me to pray even as their team prayed for me.

In due course of time amidst all the glitter, rituals and lectures from my parents on how I should not get influenced by everything I hear on radio, I was married off.

What I felt was of no consequence. What I wanted to do with my life and dreams was a non-issue.

My mother's last words to me were, " Now you have to manage your married life. Your husband's home is your home. Be good."

Husband. A stranger I had been tied to for life. I could not believe this. All my dreams were shattered. I could see my life coming to an end.

With great trepidation, I met my husband on the wedding night.

Seeing me shaking like a leaf, he tried to make me feel comfortable. I was very hesitant but he, being older than me, assuaged all my fears when he talked about my education.

"Would you like to study further?", he asked.

Slowly, he got me talking.

As the hours of our first night together passed, I began to relax in his presence and took a good look at him. He looked kind.

Gathering all my guts, I said to him, " I do not wish to hide anything from you. I have been listening to some radio programs and through one of them I have found Jesus. I trust in Him."

"What?" he exclaimed.

Scared, I looked at him as he laughed and folded his hands, saying, "I too am a follower of Jesus."

Both of us had been secret Christians but our families did not know. This was such a God moment. I wept and together we knelt down beside our marital bed to thank God for bringing us together.

We are happily married and have moved out of our joint family home and told every one about our change of faith. We face persecution but are standing strong. We share about your radio broadcast with our neighbours in this area.

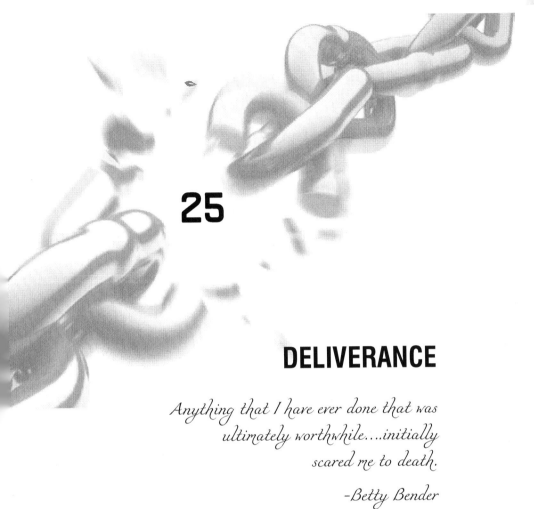

# 25

## DELIVERANCE

*Anything that I have ever done that was*
*ultimately worthwhile....initially*
*scared me to death.*

*-Betty Bender*

**"The village doctor** has been summoned yet again.

Here he comes with a dry skull and a bag containing all kinds of brooms to beat me up.

I cringe in fear and in pain.

This is my fate.

I am told that I am cursed. Although I have been married for nine years, I remain barren. We live in the deep *countryside where electricity is as much a rare visitor as the town bus.*

On most days, I felt very, very tired. Day in and out, I was cursed by my family and neighbours. They practised all kinds of magic on me hoping I would conceive. When I would get upset and angry with their actions, they would cast me aside calling me a witch. I had lost my appetite, as a result, I would fall down unconscious.

Then my head would begin to spin and my hair start flying all around me. When this would happen, the villagers would fall down and worship me saying, "The goddess has descended."

Nobody, absolutely nobody, understood my trauma. I was married at a very tender age. In the rural culture that I come from, it is normal for girls as young as 10-12 years to be married.

My husband works in the field. Being childless is considered a curse in our culture. Often, my husband threatened to leave me saying, "I will get another woman and throw you out." I lived in constant fear of rejection. He spent a lot of money on me in the hope that I would bear a child, but all in vain. I felt helpless and abused. I roamed around aimlessly in the village—hopeless and depressed.

My mother-in-law would sit under the banyan tree in our courtyard and curse me all day. I couldn't blame her. Even in her old age, she has to manage all the cooking, fetching water and cleaning all by herself.

One day, a lady in my village introduced me to a radio broadcast that airs in the morning saying, "Why don't you tune in to this program? It is possible that you may get some help from it." I went home and pulled out our little radio from a dusty drawer. Our little house is far from clean. How can I keep my house clean? My depression keeps me from performing even the basic household chores. I blew the dust off the radio and switch it on. It came alive; the signal is strong and clear. I made a note of the timing of the broadcast for the next morning, and began listening to the Christian radio broadcast that talked about Jesus.

The message I heard filled my heart with hope. At some point in the program, the gentle voice of the announcer said, "Do call us if you wish to talk to us." I could feel hope welling inside me. Yes, I wanted to talk. No harm, I thought, in trying out this option. Anyway, we had exhausted all other options.

One day, my husband got back from work. I told him about the radio program, "I guess there is no harm in talking to these people and listening to this program." He agreed.

I called on the telephone number provided at the end of the broadcast. I shared my plight with the counselor. She listened patiently and told me about Jesus. "If you trust in Jesus, He will open your womb," she said. I agreed to give it a try.

I placed my trust in Jesus and began praying in His name. I listened to the radio broadcast regularly. Within two months, I conceived.

I went for a pregnancy test, and the doctor said that the baby was fine.

We were dumbfounded. The news spreads like wildfire. My mother-in-law and husband also began listening to the radio program and praying with me. They began to care for me. My appetite returned.

We regularly called the radio counselor for prayer.

But soon, I got possessed again. It was like a fit. I was thrown and thrashed around. Those watching said that some invisible power was throwing me down and assaulting me. I was rushed to the doctor.

Fearing damage to the foetus, the doctor suggested to abort the child. I cannot believe my ears. It was unthinkable. I wailed. We waited nine years for this baby.

I called the radio counselor for prayer. She comforted me, "Trust in the Lord Jesus. He has given you this child. He will keep the child from all harm. We are praying for you. Do not worry".

I decided against aborting the child. I am trusting in Jesus to give me a normal and healthy child. We have thrown out of our house all kinds of objects we worshipped earlier. Now, we are only looking to Jesus to give me a safe delivery.

I tell many people about your radio broadcasts and how I got deliverance. Many are listening and coming to me.

Recently, I got in touch with other listeners in my area.

We are planning to meet and starting a little prayer group.

Thank you for teaching us the Truth."

# 26

# MAD

*You must be the change you wish
to see in the world.*

-MAHATMA GANDHI

**My sister's shrieking** woke me up. She was best at it.
Shrieking.

"Wake up. It's time to go to school."

I squinted opened my eyes as she put the lights on.

"It's past 5.30 a.m. and you will get me late for school
once again.

Every time because of you I get scolding," she continued
with her banter.

I was in grade 11 and my younger sister was in grade 9. I cycled to school every day with her pillion-riding.

Being a teenager, I liked to hang out with my neighbourhood friends late into the night and hence found it very difficult to wake up the next morning.

"Are you getting up or shall I call father to come and throw cold water on you?" she shrieked again.

This was the routine every school morning in our home. Sundays, I had the luxury of sleeping till late afternoon. Due to the company of my friends, who my father considered bad for me, my grades suffered. To make it worse, due to late arrival at school, my sister and I both were summoned and threatened by the school management every other week which really bothered my sister.

She was a good kid but what could I possibly do. I was young and not particularly interested in studies.

With my friends, I liked to hang out and watch cinema, stalk girls and smoke. The peer pressure was such that once I had even tasted alcohol but my father's threat to throw me out of the house did not permit me to try again. The smell had given me away.

Amidst my sister's shrieking, my mother's nagging and my father's howling, I, all of seventeen year old, plodded on with my life.

There was so much to see out there in the world, waiting for me.

I had plans. I loved taking selfies and uploading it on different modelling sites hoping that someone, somewhere could discover me and my handsome looks and give me a break.

But no such thing was happening.

Finally, when my sister shrieked for the third time, I pulled myself out of my bed and got ready in a hurry.

One day, instead of my sister's shrieks and my father's threats, a devotional program was switched on. I was surprised.

"I hope that the morning devotional program would put some good sense into your head", thundered my father and since that day, every morning the radio became my alarm clock.

Was it better than my sister's shrieking? To an extent yes. It woke me out of my delicious deep slumber, but I still considered it to be an intrusion.

One morning, I heard a broadcast that was different from the other devotional shows. I actually felt attracted to it. A sweet gentle voice read some portions from the Bible which tugged at my heart. I sensed peace. Finding it very odd, I noted the name of the broadcast.

I heard it once again the next week.

And then again and continued listening, till I became so fond of it that to my family's shock, began to wake up before the broadcast, get ready for school and actually take notes from the radio program.

Also, I began to behave myself and my family began to notice the change in me.

Time passed and I began to do well in school, reach on time with my sister.

I finished school with good grades and have now opened a coaching centre where I teach children. I am earning a decent living and also pursuing graduation through distance education.

However, there is something that still makes my family angry when I put my favourite radio program on loudspeaker for all to hear. "Have you gone mad?" they yell at me.

Not only that, I have printed the broadcast name and timings and distributed it all over the city so that others can also listen to the words of Jesus and experience the transformation that I have experienced.

My family and friends all consider me to be mad, but I am so grateful for this life-changing program because of which I am a totally new person.

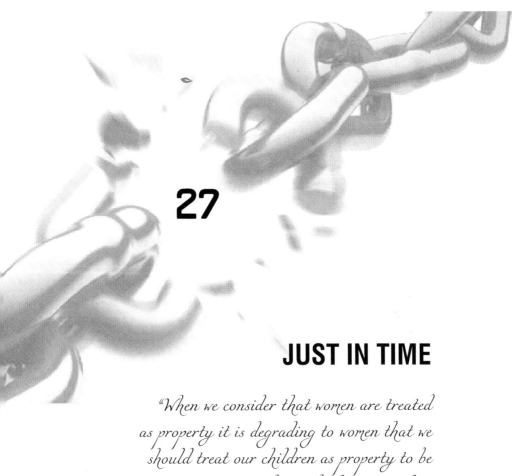

# 27

## JUST IN TIME

*"When we consider that women are treated*
*as property it is degrading to women that we*
*should treat our children as property to be*
*disposed of as we see fit."*
– ELIZABETH CADY STANTON

**I was very** nervous.

This was our third baby. We have two little girls and my mother desperately wanted us to have a son to carry on the family name.

My wife Arti was equally nervous. Although, we both belonged to a large city and both were working in multinational companies, the pressure for us to have a male child was immense.

We had been married for five years. We both worked in the same company and fell in love. Since we hail from different parts of India, with great difficulty, our parents had accepted our alliance.

Living in a big city where rubbing shoulders with people in public transport was a way of life and caste-system which is still prevalents in the rural areas, but no longer so in the cities where people thronged for higher education and jobs. Like-wise, inter-culture marriages was also fast becoming a norm. I am a Punjabi while my wife is a Bengali.

We both were doing well financially and had recently bought a car. We got along well and there was peace at home. My mother lived with us and took care of our little girls. If there was one thing that bothered us, it was my mother's persistence nagging for us to have a son.

She would often bring up the topic of having a son, which pained my wife and disturbed our relationship.

"You must have a son. How else will you get to heaven? The first two times, it did not work out, but you should try again," she insisted.

"I am afraid. What if we have a third daughter?" my wife would say to me when we were alone.

"We can always get a scan done and abort if its a girl," my mom would say to me when I would communicate my wife's fears.

"But that is illegal!" I would exclaim to which she would retort, " You keep out of this. I will work it out. I have friends and we can find out in code language if the baby is a male or a female and no one would be wiser."

"What if your parents had aborted you?", I would argue with my mother. "You are also a woman."

"We did not have scan machines in those days. Now, there are such good scan machines. Why not avail of the facilities available instead of carrying an un-wanted pregnancy for nine months," she would incessantly argue back.

Finally, she won and here I was, nervously walking in the corridor.

We were at a private hospital and my wife and mother-in-law were inside getting the scan done.

It was late night. There was hardly any one around. Some one known to my mother was helping us to determine the sex of the baby and due to her pressure, we had given in.

My mother came out of the room with a long face.

"Its again a girl. We have to abort her. You can try again after some time. You both are still young."

My pale-looking wife came out of the scan room, as white as a sheet.

I comforted her and we headed back home.

On the way back home, my mother's and wife's depression was contagious and unbearable.

To lighten our moods, I put on the local music station. Amidst some contemporary music, a radio broadcast began to talk about the adverse effects abortion has on a woman.

Least expecting the radio to play the same topic that I wanted to not think of, a woman, in detail talked about the physical, mental and emotional hazards of abortion which put the woman's life at great risk.

We listened in stunned silence.

To make it worse, the woman on the broadcast said, "God is the Life-giver and by aborting the child, we are committing a grave sin in the eyes of God. Moreover, many a times the scan reports are incorrect due to which many people end up aborting a healthy male child. Further, following abortions of baby girls, many women given birth to retarded sons."

That did it.

My mother changed her mind, sought our forgiveness and accepted our third child.

Only time would prove if it was going to be a male or a female.

During the course of the pregnancy, we regularly heard the weekly radio broadcasts on gender-equality and how women hold the key to a transformed nation. I can tell you that by listening to this broadcast, our mindset totally changed. We were ready to accept whatever God was giving us, be it male or female child. I can assure you that any one who listens to your broadcast for three times, will be a changed person.

A third daughter was born to us and we have accepted her. She is a normal child and we are very grateful.

We have promised ourselves to give the best opportunities we can, to our three girls.

Your broadcast has saved us from a grievous sin. Not only would be have killed our baby girl but also put my wife in grave danger.

———✦———

57435368R00086

Made in the USA
San Bernardino, CA
19 November 2017